TOP DOWN ANALYSIS ON THE FINANCIAL MARKETS

REF WAYNE &
BAFANA MASILELA

CONTENTS

FOREWORD

Even though I wrote the best seller - The Art of Trading – myself, I have to admit that I was quite nervous working on this book. Not only was it the first time I was co-authoring a book, but my co-author was in fact a longstanding mentor, and when I saw the first draft of the content I knew I had to up my game.

Before I get onto the book, let me introduce my mentor, friend, co-author and trader extraordinaire - Bafana Masilela. We were fortunate to be introduced on Facebook by another brilliant trader, Vusi Mtsweni. We hit it off immediately and spent hours on the phone discussing and debating various strategies and subjects.

That was about a decade ago - when Forex Trading was less visible, more underground. There were no flashy cars or Instagram millionaires flaunting their bling-bling lifestyle. You could literally count the traders on both hands. I remember trying to create a Mastermind Traders Group, but this was a dismal failure in Johannesburg and achieved marginal success in Durban.

While it was harder and tougher back then, watching Bafana Masilela in action, leading the way and contributing to raising Forex literacy, knowledge and understanding was a blessing. I personally experienced the pivotal role Bafana played and the contributions he made to the growth and resurgence of the industry.

In early 2020, when Bafana contacted me and told me he needed some advice on a book he was writing, I knew right away that I wanted to contribute and collaborate on the book. And no way was I missing an opportunity to collaborate with Bafana again.

At the time, we had no idea about the impending pandemic, and the devastation it would wreak on livelihoods and economies around the world.

More so now than ever, we need to find a new way to earn and make a better income.

This book is written for the professional trader that is sick and tired of making money then losing it all. I'm taking about the hungry trader – the trader who wants to master the art of winning far more times than losing, the trader who want to know more and is driven to uncover the secrets to making it big.

If you are a novice and have a good understanding then there are plenty of nuggets you'll find, but if you're a beginner – I recommend you read my first book – The Art of Trading.

You will notice that the book is divided in two parts. The first part covers the mindset a successful trader needs to adopt. The second part focuses on trading strategies written by Bafana.

We hope you enjoy the book, may it bring you success and wealth. Shaayaa!

Ref Wayne

Forex Master and Author of The Art of Trading
Johannesburg, South Africa

INTRODUCTION

Foreign Exchange (FOREX) Trading has grown enormously and is becoming more popular by the day - especially in Africa. This excites and thrills me as my dream has always been to show other people that there is another way to make a living. A smarter way that equips you to create a life you want, unlimited by circumstances and self-limiting beliefs about what you can achieve. Working hard for someone else, very seldom leads to financial freedom and success.

Since the COVID-19 pandemic hit, working from home has become the new normal. Flexi-work is now globally accepted and understood. Prior to this, Africans never understood the concept of working from home as their job was to hunt, and that certainly wasn't possible from home. In addition, up until recently, most Africans were blue collar workers.

Currency trading is an international trading market where financial institutions like banks, insurance companies, hedge funds, businesses and public and private investors obtain and exchange currencies. Unlike the stock market that operates only at fixed times, forex trading doesn't close, running 24 hours a day, 5 days a week. It is estimated that the FOREX market has an estimated trading volume of $5 trillion, making it the most lucrative marketplace in the world. Due to the depth and liquidity of the market, Forex is regarded as the world's largest currency trading market.

In this book, you will discover both the psychological mindset as well as the knowledge, skills and strategies that separate winners from losers, strategists from gamblers, cowboys from gamechangers. My recipe for a winning mindset is a blend of careful analysis and effective implementation. It is applicable in every aspect of human endeavour.

As an instructor, a healthcare provider, an entrepreneur and a strategist; I know first-hand how analysis and implementation are necessary for success. No trader meets their target without doing a careful analysis of the environment and market trends first so that the right trade, at the right time is identified and implemented.

Once an exclusive activity reserved for governments, commercial and investment banks, and public investors, Forex Trading is now open to private and retail traders like us. I for one, feel extremely privileged to participate in this marketplace and succeed beyond my wildest dreams. We hope this book equips many more traders to succeed more often.

Part 1

TRADING PSYCHOLOGY

by Ref Wayne

The psychological element is as important as the 2nd part of this book, it forms the framework and serves as a building block around implementing your strategies on the market. Unfortunately, this element is often overlooked. In this part, we delve deeper into discovering your hidden enemies and obstacles to your trading success.

1. EQUI-LIBRIUM

The market is ruled by forces that are in constant equilibrium - you just have to know one thing about the market and that is WHERE it will turn. If you know when the market is going to turn, you will be profitable. And in order to know when the market will turn, you need to understand the forces behind the market and market makers.

Top Down Analysis or Multi-Time Frame Analysis is an imperative rule - my mentor first taught me that as a trader you need to always use at least 2 timeframes - a longer and a shorter timeframe. By helping you to find precise entry and exit points, this approach keeps you a few steps ahead.

Depending on your style of trading I recommend that you combine the following timeframes that I refer to as Forex Chords. The reason I call them chords is because just like you can find in music, harmony is created when they are used together. Notes when played together are called chords. In other words, at the deepest level of trading, it's as natural as harmonious music.

- 5 minutes works with 30 minutes TF

- 15 minutes works with 1-hour TF

- 1 hour works with 4-hour TF

- 4 hour works with daily TF

In my book The Art of Trading, I taught that:

SCALPING

Requires tact, speed and quick wit. The timeframe to trade this style is the 30-, 15-, 5- and 1-minute charts. Use these charts to see the overall direction of the entire flow.

INTRA-DAY TRADING

Is the style used by the trader who opens trades that are to be closed before the end of the day. The recommended charts for this style are the 1 Hour and the 30 Minutes charts.

POSITION TRADING

Makes it possible for long-term traders to spend only a few minutes analysing the market and profit in the long run. They usually hold trades longer than a day and some even take profit after months in the position – depending on how well they had forecasted the traded pair.

So, in Top Down Analysis we teach that you MUST always start from the higher time frame and go down with it! Using this method will help you understand how the market operates under various mechanisms of exchange, which affect liquidity and control.

2. YOUR ENEMIES

Luck never lasts but skill does. To be a consistent and profitable trader, you need mental stamina and a razor sharp mind. You also need to approach it with a clear focused mind free from stress and other issues. Like any endeavour, forex should be treated as a business, it's not a casino where luck rules the day, its 80% mindset and 20% actual strategy.

You can have the best strategy and still blow your account, so your mindset must be in the right place. People who approach the market looking for a lucky break often end up experiencing bad luck. You see, it's the mind of the broker that can be the real enemy. Dealing with your mindset early on, is the first step you need to take. Remember I am not teaching you any strategies, I am just preparing you for 2nd part of the book.

Every forex trading book will say that you must trade on a demo first, this book presents a different view. It encourages you to start trading on a real account as soon as possible because we know that is where you will learn mastery over your emotions and understand the psychological side of trading quicker. It is emotionally more profitable to trade on a real account even if it's as little as US$50 - trust me, it's so much better than a million on a demo. While you can test a few strategies on a demo, having a real account is a must if you are want to master your emotions.

The biggest threat and greatest hindrance to success in trading is **Overconfidence**. I have always said that the market will humble you, it's a great teacher of humility. I hate to see traders becoming cocky after a few wins. My signal members can testify that this year has been our best year so far with a remarkable 98% win rate yet I remain humble because I know that the minute I become cocky then my emotions will cloud my judgement. I don't like being put on a pedestal – for me relaxation is key.

The minute you are overconfident, you will start over trading and from there it's only going to get worse. From over trading to revenge trading - this is when the ego is completely taking you for a ride – it doesn't want you to accept a loss, so it keeps going back in and in again, until you are bust.

The second enemy is **Greed** – and the trader must overcome this hurdle in the early stages or they can suffer from the consequences of not taking profit, wanting more and not respecting their daily targets. As they say winners know when to stop.

Fear is another enemy and the market deals with fearful traders in very harsh ways – it's almost as if it can smell fear. Of course, there is a fine line between fearful and overconfident traders. Finding the right balance is critical. Be confident but not overconfident, but avoid fear, enter a trade calmly.

Jealousy is the final enemy and one that is really hurting local traders. Remember there is more than enough money for all traders to take from the market so there's no reason to get caught up in petty jealousies. Interestingly, these traders are always dealt with somehow by the market.

2. WINNING PSYCHOLOGY RECIPE

When you learn and understand the pros and cons of trading, forex markets are sources of exciting and profitable financial adventures. It is easier to think that your trader pals are making easy money when you see them cashing out big.

Honestly, the forex markets are lucrative platforms for trading, but only if you understand the psychology of buying and selling currencies. That's why learning how to strategise is as important as understanding the key points of forex trading. The key takeaway enables you to strategise and implement. Thus, understanding the risk involved and having the right skill sets (which include talent, discipline, and training) enables you to strategise effectively. This is the hallmark of my Winning Psychology Recipe.

Interest is the first factor to consider before venturing into anything. After interest comes talent. Although everyone might not have the talent to do a certain thing, their ability to develop the right attitude and being able to strategise will shoot them to the apex of their career. This brings us to the crux of this chapter: learning how to strategise by implementing my Winning Psychology Recipe.

DEVELOPING A WINNER'S MINDSET

No one becomes a winner without developing the mindset to win. In the scheme of things, there are observers and performers. Observers are not so keen on becoming successful, performers represent success, and they become successful through strategising. In forex trading, maintaining discipline is not only necessary but a key aspect of trading. Globally celebrated successful forex traders have a mindset enabled by the following:

1. Self-discipline, which is their ability to understand when a certain trade is wrong and keep away from it to minimize losses.

2. Ability to assess and proffer risk-control measures. They understand the importance of taking risks, but they also understand that not all risks are worth it. They study the trade to differentiate between attendant risks and rewards.

3. Sheer courageousness. Winners are goal-getters, and no successful person created a legacy without being courageous. Behind every courageous person is a legacy, and behind every legacy is a legend. Those who have been identified as successful forex traders are legends. They understand the fears and scepticism of others yet they dare to succeed. They strive to be different from naysayers, observers, and bystanders. They strive to be the legend behind the legacy.

4. They are shrewd business people. Every successful forex trader is ruthless in their business dealings. They aren't ruthless because they do shady deals but because they are different from the ordinary business person. Their astuteness differentiates them from those who lack self-discipline. They study the markets to understand how financial movements are shaping market trends.

5. They learn from their mistakes. Successful people do not see themselves as masters of the game. They try to master the market, but they aren't masters of the market. There is a difference between the two. While those who think they've got the knowledge try to blank out information, those who have mastered their market know that there could be something to take from every conversation.

"FAILURE WILL NEVER OVERTAKE ME IF MY DETERMINATION TO SUCCEED IS STRONG ENOUGH."

Og Mandino

Thus, if they hear that there is going to be a decline in the price of oil or gold, they don't push the information aside. Rather, they will try to verify it because they know that it determines the next move they are going to make. They don't try to prove to themselves that they have ample knowledge of the market; they tell themselves to be open to gather knowledge about the market.

These are factors that define winners, and every successful forex trader possesses these traits. What do Paul Tudor Jones, Buddy Fletcher, and Ref Wayne have in common? Apart from being recognized as some of the most successful forex traders, they didn't get to the apex of their career by lounging around; they achieved tremendous success because they pursued their business with the level of tenacity that I have grouped under the ingredients that make up the Winning Psychology Recipe: talent, discipline, and training.

The Winning Psychology Recipe is built on awareness. The successful person is aware of their weaknesses and their strengths. They are aware of their goals and vision. They are aware of the process of actualizing these goals, and they are aware of the patterns of the process. They are aware of eminent adversity, and they are prepared with the right tools to fight their way to victory.

They are aware that despite the feasibility of the processes, they should always double-check the process for changes and loopholes. There are a few ingredients that go into formulating the recipe of a winner's mindset. Frankly, these ingredients are many and will be mentioned throughout the book. Here, I will discuss the tools required to develop a winner's mindset:

1. Patience: Successful forex traders have patience as a common virtue. This is not peculiar to them alone. Most business people who aim to succeed embrace patience. As a newbie in the FX markets, your ability to distinguish the moment to be patient, and the time to act is your first move towards success. If you study your market well and understand what to expect from your system, the winner's mindset tells you to be patient.

2. Discipline: No one achieves anything in life if they are not disciplined. Discipline comes in two forms - you could be disciplined in the way you relate to people and in the way you relate to yourself. The thing is, both work well together. If you focus on self-discipline without watching how you relate to others, the activities of others might ruin what you have worked hard for. You cannot be patient if you aren't disciplined. Successful forex traders do not get to the top of their careers without being disciplined with themselves and with their trades.

3. Objectivity: Your objectivity and ability to trust your system are necessary for success in the FX markets. Most successful business people begin to record landslide success the moment they learn the art of emotional detachment. It is not an easy feat, but it's achievable. Many businesses failed because the people involved were unable to master their emotions and control negative energy coming from internal and external factors. One needs to learn how not to be influenced by the opinions of pundits. Although one should take suggestions into consideration, one mustn't base their financial decisions on them. During the preparation stage, successful forex traders identify the most reliable system and act on their signals with confidence.

4. Feasible expectations: Even though successful forex traders trade with the confidence that their trading acumen will yield huge profit, they know they have to be realistic with their expectations. They don't entertain the piper's dream of making a profit of $1,500 per trade when they invested $300 in their trading account. They know that even though the markets can change, they should expect practical return on investment (ROI).

5. Risk assessment: Successful forex traders are conscious of risk; which is why they make contingency plans to cushion the effects of any foreseeable risk. This is known as the ability to control risks. Risk control is the process of evaluating potential losses and subsequent interventions to reduce or eliminate possible risks. That's why even though traders evaluate potential losses and make actionable plans to reduce them, they also create a proviso that reduces the outcome of the risks on their profit.

Developing a winner's mindset is the first step towards success. People engage in different ventures, but their success story is facilitated by one thing: a winner's mindset. Successful forex traders understand the makeup of legends and they know that success is not a birth right. It is not the outcome of luck. Rather, success is built. It is created through discipline, tenacity, patience, objectivity and focus. As American Billionaire, Warren Buffet, states so succinctly –

"There are two rules in trading. The first rule is to never lose money and the second rule is to remember rule number one."

4. PREPARE & STRATEGIZE

Successful forex traders develop and implement strategies that boost their activities and success in the markets. They understand how important developing the right strategy is and when they develop one, they work to implement it. Apart from having the talent to do business , forex traders approach trading professionally. Trading currencies requires consistency, attentiveness, and discipline. Successful forex traders understand these factors and they work with them.

Before investing in the business, smart traders understand the need for preparation. They begin to prepare by aligning their financial and economic goals alongside their personal idiosyncrasies within the framework of relatable instruments and markets. This way, they gather the right knowledge regarding what to trade-in. This will be narrowed down for more clarification.

For example, if a trader has expert knowledge of retail markets, it makes so much more sense to venture into trading retail stocks as opposed to oil or gold futures. Sometimes, newbies in forex trading make mistakes or take risks that boomerang. They don't do this deliberately (after all no sane person makes a calculated attempt to lose money). Most times, the reason for the miscalculation is misinformation or lack of experience.

Before venturing into any business, calculated and shrewd businesspeople check the socio-economic derivatives of the business they want to invest in. This is called preparation, and preparation is one of the ingredients in the Winning Psychology Recipe. When you understand the viability of the commodity you want to invest in, it becomes easier to foresee the gains or losses inherent in the venture. If a guru in retail markets decides to branch out into oil futures without understudying the environment surrounding the business, they might lose huge funds by investing in what they do not understand. That's why preparation is important. Successful traders do not jump into the markets and begin trading immediately; they survey the financial and economic landscapes before they invest.

Because of the tendencies to attach low commissions and fees, the forex markets can be accessed by private investors. What that means is that a lot of people can venture into it. This increases the opportunity to make more profit but at the same time, shrinks the opportunity to become successful through it. The acceptability and participation of a large number of people make the FX markets the largest financial exchange market. Thus, without adequate knowledge and proper preparation, some traders are likely to lose money to those who are prepared before venturing. To venture into the markets, successful traders take their level of understanding of the business seriously. Simply said, they do their due diligence.

So, before you go too far, you must have a solid understanding of what the markets are doing and how to navigate them. Knowledge and understanding of the pros and cons of the markets are part of the psychological makeup of successful forex traders. As understanding and implementation are the ingredients that make up the preparation recipe, forex traders become successful by taking note of the following components:

1. They work within a strategic timeframe: This ingredient works inwardly and outwardly simultaneously. Strategising according to the timeframe focuses on the traits and business acumen of the trader. This indicates the sort of trading suitable for the talents and experience of the trader. Successful traders do not overlook this.

Say Trader A loves trading off 1 Hour charts - this timeframe indicates that they prefer taking a position within the landscape they are familiar with, without being exposed to overnight risks. And to prevent or minimise loss, they weigh their strengths and work with what they have discovered. But if Trader B prefers

Weekly charts, they are comfortable with overnight risks. Thus, the 1 Hour and Weekly charted traders have mastered their timeframe according to their ability. And if they maintain this, there will be few occurrences of losses. This is what it means to get prepared according to the timeframe.

2. They create and work with a practical system: Successful forex traders work with a methodology. Once they have established their favourable timeframes, they choose a consistent methodology. This is one of the secrets of success.

Let's use the traders we met above. Whereas Trader A prefers a 1 Hour chart timeframe, Trader B favours weekly charts. If Trader A wants to record more success when compared to other traders trading within the same chart timeframe, they have to create a methodology. Now, this is about having an established system or pattern of trading. For example, some traders prefer to buy support and sell resistance, while others prefer to buy or sell breakouts or trade using indicators like MACD (moving average convergence divergence) and crossovers.

These methodologies are good, but they become profitable when the trader understands the peculiarities of each. The understanding helps them make an informed decision on the methodology to use. And if you study this according to the preparation recipe, such traders become successful if they blend methodology with consistency. But choosing a methodology is one piece of the pie. Finding an edge is the next step to take after choosing a methodology. This is how successful forex traders do it. Once they find a system that works, they test it over time. And if after a certain attempt they discover that it worked more than 50% of the time, they mark it as "an edge", which is a pattern that produces a consistently positive outcome. When expert traders test a system and they discover it produces consistent positive outcomes more than others, they stick to it. So be sure to learn and study the second part of this book thoroughly so that your strategy is rock solid.

3. They work with the best market: No successful forex trader knows how to work best with the market without subjecting themselves to constant training. In preparation, training is indispensable. Training enables traders to discover the particular market (otherwise known as instruments) that trades systematically and more orderly than others. They do so because working with just any system might jeopardise their chances to be successful. If we study the trends in these markets, we will discover that some unstable trading instruments delay or even stall the possibility of having a winning system. Successful traders don't rely on luck to get the result they want. They are proactive when working with key factors and they use their initiative to create a balance. This is how they achieve success. Successful forex traders test their system on tonnes of instruments for a reason. This is to determine if their system's style is compatible with the instrument they are trading. For example, if Trader B is trading USD/JPY currency pair in the market, they are likely to discover that Fibonacci support and resistance levels are more reliable and compatible with their instrument than other system styles. In line with the strategies taught in this book, I recommend you trade the major currency pairs: EUR/USD, USD/JPY, AUD/USD and GBP/USD (my favourite).

Preparation is one of the key ingredients of the Winning Psychology Recipe that makes forex traders successful. It enables them to choose the most reliable and compatible system style for their instruments. If a trader understands the financial trends in the markets but they pair their trading instruments with the wrong system style, there is a higher chance they will be less successful. Therefore, to avoid failure even with talent, preparation needs to meet with strategy. Strategising is core of the Winning Psychology Recipe. It is the cache that harbours the characteristics of a winner. We will see how this works in the next chapter.

5. CHARACTERISTICS OF A WINNER

In every human venture and adventure, there is a thing that differentiates the reason for, or the outcome of activities carried out in point A with those carried out in point B.

A drug offender might serve a prison term in the UK (depending on the weight of their crime), while someone who committed a similar crime might face the gallows in countries with extreme drug laws, such as Thailand, Indonesia, China, or Myanmar. Many countries have declared war on drugs, but not all countries are insisting on mass incarceration and execution like some South Asian countries. This demonstrates the use of different strategies, and it is replicated in other socioeconomic aspects of humans.

For the outcomes of the winning psychology or the lack of it, the difference lies in what separates performers from observers.

Performers are always eager to come up with new performances. They do not want their energy to deplete and they always prepare or train themselves to give their best in any situation. This would explain why you would see an artist working on their canvas every day despite any exhibition time pressure. But this is not the case with observers.

Observers wait for an exhibition before they begin to prepare. There is nothing wrong with being an observer, but when a performer becomes an observer, it reduces their active participation.

An observer might also be a performer, but no serious performer will be an observer unless they want to sit back to revel in the outcome of their performance. In this case the observer-performer aims to create the same outcomes the active-performer creates, but the difference between them is their goal.

The observer-performer worries about the outcome more than they are concerned with the process. But the active-performer is more concerned with the process; rather than the outcome, because they know that when the process is right, the outcome will be right. This can be explained through the process of building wealth and tax evasion using Robert Kiyosaki's Cash Flow Quadrant.

Robert Kiyosaki's Cash Flow Quadrant has two segments and four categories. The four categories are divided into two to fit into the two segments: left and right.

The two segments are known as The Poor Dad's Cash Flow Quadrant (left) and The Rich Dad's Cash Flow Quadrant (right).

The Poor Dad's Cash Flow Quadrant (left) represents the "E" (employee) and the "S" (self-employed). Employees work the hardest; earn very little compared to the people on the right and pay the most tax. They need to work harder and harder to earn more money to keep up with the rising cost of living. And when one job isn't giving them what they need, they look for another and the cycle continues. And if you're self-employed, it's not any easier. Very often self-employed means running a one-man business where they often believe they are the only ones who can keep their business afloat and therefore refrain from delegating duties to anyone. In the long run, when the owner is not available, the business suffers the consequences of their absence - often lying dormant with slim chances of generating cash flow.

The right side of Rich Dad's Cash Flow Quadrant represents the "B" (business owner) and the "I" (investor). These people are smart money-makers because they understand what it takes to grow sustainable cashflow. What they do is hire people who have more skill than them to run their business, and thereby delegate the business' operations. Although business owners can be risk-takers, not all investors necessarily run the daily operations of any business. Business owners and investors grow their business by investing in ventures that generate consistent cashflow, and these ventures, in turn, give them assets. The assets generate more money and the investor acquires additional assets with the money generated. This way their money grows in vast measures, they have time to themselves, and might even choose not to do any active work for a long time. They pay less tax or might even not pay any since the taxing system focuses on taxing active income. The "I" and the "B" mostly avoid tax and take less risk because their money comes from investments. Monies generated through investment are grouped under passive income.

Investors and Business owner are active-performers, while employees and the self-employed are observer-performers.

Winners and successful forex traders are proactive and have initiative as well. Unlike those in other fields (such as the healthcare system) whose goal can be outcome based, forex traders know that the process determines the outcome. Thus, they understand that there is no destination. They work hard to get their desired results and they continue to work smart to maintain the success they have achieved. This journey to success is not easy, but it is achievable.

Mindset is another aspect of the Winning Psychology Recipe and it is not inherited at birth. An aspirant trader might train under an expert broker, but if they lack the right mindset that that leads to success, they will be far less successful than their mentor. Let's break this down. Success is not handed down to anyone, nor is a growth mindset. Someone might be successful at a time, but if they have a fixed mindset, they are likely to function like someone who is self-employed and unable to generate steady cash flow because they were not in the right mindset. For the trader with a fixed mindset, their success will be short-lived. Thus, the first idea to take away is that success and mindset are not handed down. They are developed and worked for. Characteristics of a winner and indicators of the Winning Psychology Recipe are:

1. The ability to differentiate talent and expertise: Great entrepreneurs have the entrepreneurial spirit (which is talent), but they don't rely on it alone. They polish it. Everyone is good at something, but few reach great heights. David Beckham wasn't the only boy from his neighbourhood who loved playing soccer, but he was one of the few to become successful because he turned his passion into a business. Mindset changes everything. Beckham became successful because he understood that the mindset that differentiates a hobby from a business is developed through discipline, drive, effort and commitment. So even though a trader might be naturally talented with numbers, they understand that learning and practise are required to make their talent yield big results.

2. The ability to build grit and guts: Success is a concept, but being successful is an action. When people desire to be successful, they indulge in activities that make them successful. But oftentimes, the actionable information that gave them their success story is rarely the one that keeps them successful. Remaining successful requires something else, and that is tenacity, also known as grit. Successful people utilise grit and guts, instead of talent and luck, to become more successful. Tenacity is a characteristic of successful forex traders and an indicator of achievement. Grit and guts are a combination of courage, passion and perseverance utilised to achieve a definite goal.

Renowned people like Isaac Newton and Albert Einstein had talent. They were born with an IQ higher than most. But they didn't rely on their talent alone. They harnessed the potentials of their innate gifts alongside their tendencies for growth to become great achievers. This is the same thing successful forex traders do. They have mastered the art of winning and through this knowledge they devise ways to succeed. Grit and guts are ingredients that help winners turn setbacks into strategic wins.

3. The ability to be impetuous: Impetus is a trait found in winners. Successful people don't wait around for the right moment. They take a moment and make it the right moment for the business. Turning any moment into the right moment does not in any way promote mindlessness. It champions audaciousness and momentum. Impetuous forex traders generate momentum that propels them in the right direction. They are smart people who do not believe in happenstance. If the forex markets are tumultuous, they know the right approach to ride the wave. And they ride the wave they built during the preparation stage. During preparation, they established their goal. And since their goal isn't about the outcome but the process, they proceed through the process carefully. As such, when the journey becomes a bumpy ride, they don't lose momentum because they are following a prepared process.

4. The ability to trust their vision: Arnold Schwarzenegger, the celebrated bodybuilder, actor and former governor of California told the story of how he achieved so much success. In his story, he revealed that the problem most people face or one of the hindrances to success is lack of vision. He had told the story of how his family and outsiders thought he was wasting his time training his body.

* "How To Train For Mass: Arnold Schwarzenegger's Blueprint Training Program". Retrieved on 1 September, 2020 from: www.youtube.com/watch?v=o9zCgPtsups

"IF YOU ARE WORKING ON SOMETHING THAT YOU REALLY CARE ABOUT, YOU DON'T HAVE TO BE PUSHED. THE VISION PULLS YOU."

Steve Jobs

He said: "I wasn't born rich but I wasn't poor, because I had a dream: the dream to be the greatest bodybuilder of all time. I wanted to use bodybuilding as a means to get into films." And he caps it off by saying: "Never ever dream small. If you want to accomplish anything, you have to think big and reach for the stars. Not every legend is a myth. Some are flesh and blood. Some legends walk among us. But they aren't born; they're built. Legends are made from iron and sweat, muscle, blood, and vision and victory. Legends are champions. They win. They conquer. There is a legend behind every legacy. There is a blueprint behind every legend." *(*)*

Arnold trusted his vision. He knew where he was going. He worked to get there, and he succeeded. This pertains to successful forex traders, and just like Arnold said, their goal is the blueprint behind their success. They had a vision; a dream and they stayed with it. They don't stray from their vision. They don't compromise the process. They believe in its actualisation and they continue to utilise their optimism along the way.

5. The ability to be self-sufficient and open-minded: Being self-sufficient differs from being self-absorbed. A self-sufficient business person understands the need to seek expert opinion before making a financial decision, while a self-absorbed business person make decisions before seeking expert opinion. A self-sufficient person is confident in their abilities. They are emotionally and psychologically stable, unlike the self-absorbed person who has a superior or grandiose opinion of self. Oftentimes, the self-sufficient person is more knowledgeable than the self-absorbed person.

In forex trading, a successful trader is often self-sufficient. Although they trust their ability, they do not limit themselves from learning from those who are experienced when the opportunity presents itself. Being self-sufficient and open-minded is an important ingredient in the Winning Psychology Recipe. Winners who have this psychology open their minds to positivity and shut off from negative energy. They do not allow the narrow or short-sightedness of small-minded people to deter them. They choose a goal and fix their minds on it.

6. The ability to take action: Every ingredient is powerful and necessary, but if action is lacking, there wouldn't be a legend. Action is the most vital blueprint of every legend. If you establish what to do and how to do it, but fail to generate the momentum to ignite the success story you desire, your achievements will suffer. People in the world back their vision with action. If global names like Jeff Bezos had ended his story with a vision without action, where would a global marketplace like Amazon come from? Maybe there would have been another e-commerce giant, but it wouldn't be Amazon. Today Amazon exists with other virtual markets because these successful leaders had a vision they acted upon.

The characteristics of a winner are not inborn. Although some people are born with great leadership qualities, not everyone becomes successful through these qualities. Successful leaders and businesspeople who were born with innate qualities actualised their abilities. And those who did not have any innate skill developed theirs over time.

6. MASTERY OVER EMOTIONS

Popular belief maintains that emotions are innate reactions triggered by the environment. While this could be true, it is also true that we can exercise control over what particular emotion we want to manifest. We don't experience or react to a situation in a particular way because people react to it similarly; we create our reactions based on the way we relate to the circumstance.

Each emotional reaction originates from self-constructs. This means that people construct their emotions based on their past experiences and current perception of things. They also construct through relative meanings. For instance, a businessman who experienced a downturn in his investment might become sceptical when someone brings a proposal that reminds them of that experience. The scepticism might be a direct emotional response to instincts and experience. And whether he decides to buy into the business or not, his emotions contributed to whichever decision he made. Emotions are not innate as people have been made to believe. They are constructed, and everyone has the power to reconstruct theirs.

In business, having emotional intelligence is necessary. Emotional intelligence, also known as sensitivity, helps in decision making. It is an important ingredient in the Winning Psychology Recipe. Every successful individual is required to gain mastery over their emotions to remain successful. Fear and pride are two unhealthy emotional reactions for business. During the preparation stage, if a forex trader entertains one or both of these emotions, their business will likely take a downturn. But successful forex traders understand this and they make adequate adjustments to master their emotions. They understand the feelings that lead to good business and the emotions that destroy hard work. Since they aim to win and continue winning, they develop mastery over their emotions. Emotional mastery is one of the characteristics of winning psychology, and it is incorporated into the psychology of successful forex traders.

RISK MANAGEMENT

In business, your ability to manage risk is reliant on emotional intelligence. The process of identifying, understanding, analyzing, accepting or judging uncertainty in investment decisions is known as risk management. Risk management doesn't have to be a frightening concept, unlike what some inexperienced businesspeople want others to believe. Risk management is required for a business to thrive. No shrewd businessperson engages in a business venture without assessing the level of potential losses they are going to encounter. And when they do, they take the proper action regarding what they have discovered based on their investment objectives and risk tolerance.

Risk management occurs in every level of financial dealings. In FX markets, risk assessment based on risk tolerance is necessary. No forex trader has become successful without doing an adequate risk assessment before investing in the markets. They check for risks before they trade. It is common that people think that risk is perpetually negative and should be avoided. Even though their assumptions might be valid, investments and profits cannot be discussed outside the confines of risk-taking and risk management. Risk is necessary for desirable performance, but if you want to regulate the frequency of potential risk on every trade you make, you will have to go with the strategies of successful forex traders.

Successful forex traders control how they lose money by implementing a risk management strategy. These strategies are designed to help cut down losses and protect their trading accounts from exhaustion, and they achieve these by staying focused. Staying focused is as important to risk management as doing due diligence and keeping negative emotions at bay.

Emotions are required to effectively run businesses, especially if you are in tune with your instincts. But when your instincts are consistently leading to poor choices or when a friend is persuading you to invest during a turbulent financial climate, emotions and common sense are required to make the right financial decision by carrying out a proper risk assessment. Risk management and assessment is the reason some businesspeople are more successful than others, even when they seem to invest in the same commodities. Successful forex traders understand this and they work with it.

ASSESSING AND MANAGING RISK

1. Stick to a winning trade: Although there is no definite formula for avoiding risk in business, a trader's ability to determine their trading strategy's win-loss ratio and the average size of their wins and losses are enough to manage risk. This is achieved by studying trading numbers and the sum of the long-term profitability of these numbers. And when this is clarified, it's easier to identify the winning trade and stick to it.

2. Learn how to minimize losses: This takes us back to Warren Buffet's rules of trading – "**Rule Number 1: never lose money, and Rule Number 2: never forget rule number 1**." This is the basic process of minimizing losses. Knowing how to obey rule 1 and rule 2 depends on mindset. Successful forex traders have the right mindset. They understand how to cut their losses. They learn to never lose more than 1% of their portfolio on any trade.

3. Learn to keep emotions out of business: This aspect is imperative. Involving emotions in business has never profited any business person. Even though instincts and past experiences create emotions that should be listened to, trading purely with emotions is usually disastrous. Successful traders understand this, which is why they don't delegate duties to amateurs. Expert traders understand when the system says get out, but an amateur trader will possibly hold on for bigger wins and often end up losing money.

The three points above address how successful forex traders manage risk. And through these risk management tips, they learn how to overcome negativity.

OVERCOMING NEGATIVITY

Everything about growing a big business is based on mindset: the psychology of a winner. Learning how to overcome negativity is no different. Being self-disciplined helps businesspeople tackle negativity. Negativity can come from internal or external factors. And there are times when both factors influence negativity.

A successful business is the product of hard work, talent, discipline and training. Amid these winning tendencies, negativity commonly finds a way to sneak in to ruin all the good work. Negativity is not as terrible as it has been portrayed. Honestly, negativity can be useful in saving money and cutting back on losses when a trader learns how to navigate its effects.

However, because only a few persons have learned how to monitor and control their thoughts, the smartest way remains learning how to overcome negativity. Successful forex traders know these tools and they work with them to succeed.

HOW TO OVERCOME NEGATIVITY

1. Acknowledge your plans aren't fool-proof: Most times, people work on their vision but they fail to understand that their goals need to be flexible. Anything can happen to what appeared to be a fool proof plan. When problems are not anticipated, its easy to get thrown off balance. Just remember, just as one plan can fall apart, a new plan can come into play. When you work with this mindset, you will experience less disappointment.

2. Be your own cheerleader: In business and other life ventures, there will be naysayers. There will be pessimists who will try to dissuade you from following your dreams. If you heed everything they say, the chances of becoming successful will be slim. Successful forex traders make it to the top by being self-supportive. They find strength in themselves before they look for encouragement and support from others. Once they establish that a venture is profitable and have done a quality risk assessment, they go ahead and invest.

3. Start small and gather momentum: While it is ideal to think big for your business, it is wise to work your way slowly while looking out for practical opportunities to succeed. Positivity does not entail taking mindless risks. As a forex trader, you should pay attention to the markets, fall under the mentorship of expert traders, and be open to act when your system says it's right. This was exactly what George Soros did. He was persistent and consistent. He monitored the markets. And he moved in for the kill when the opportunity was right. Moving step by step until you get to the apex of your career is the easiest way to maintain positivity.

Successful forex traders do not create room for negativity and certainly do not take mindless risks. They understand the pros and cons of their trade and, even though a business can take a downward turn when you least expect it, they trade according to what they know. They do not actively engage in known oversights and they never give up.

7. IN CONCLUSION

The Winning Psychology Recipe is the outcome of a conscious mindset. In food preparation settings, the ability to produce great meals depends on the skills of the chef. An ordinary person may cook a certain delicacy in a certain way and it would be accepted because they aren't a professional. But if a meal should meet international standards, the chef is required to master the art of preparing this delicacy to perfection.

What differentiates the meals prepared by a professional chef from those of an ordinary cook is the recipe. A recipe is a combination of talent, discipline, and training. And the makeup of these three things are known as ingredients. In the recipe for developing winning psychology, we have shown that talent is not enough. No one is born a legend. They might be born with a name or title, but they become legends through the legacy they create for themselves.

Legends are winners and they are the manifestation of the materials that make up a legacy: hard work, patience, vision, tenacity, perseverance, consistency, positivity and discipline. These are the essential aspects of success and successful forex traders have these qualities. This book has revealed what goes into developing winning psychology – and it's not a work of chance. Mindset is key. We looked at the characteristics of a winner and how these characteristics help them to win, even amid setbacks. We discussed how to deal with emotions and how mastery over emotions helps with risk management and overcoming negativity. These are all outcomes of the winning mindset of successful forex traders. I hope you have found this helpful and will facilitate future success.

Part 2

TOP DOWN ANALYSIS

by Bafana Masilela

This is where you are going to learn more about the technical side of the market. Our main focus is to equip you with enough tools to be able to understand and read the price correctly. All the chapters are like puzzles that need to be connected, which means you will need to read the whole book before you can connect the dots.

1.

REVERSAL ZONE

Lets begin by clarifying a few aspects that are already there so we can be on the same page.

The market always has turning points regardless of market sentiment or condition. We all know that the market never goes up or down forever, somewhere along the line it has to stop and reverse. An ideal reversal zone usually possesses several characteristics that clearly separate it from other types of price action.

1.1 Bullish and Bearish Reversals

a. Bullish Reversal: a currency pair converts from a downtrend to bullish sentiment.

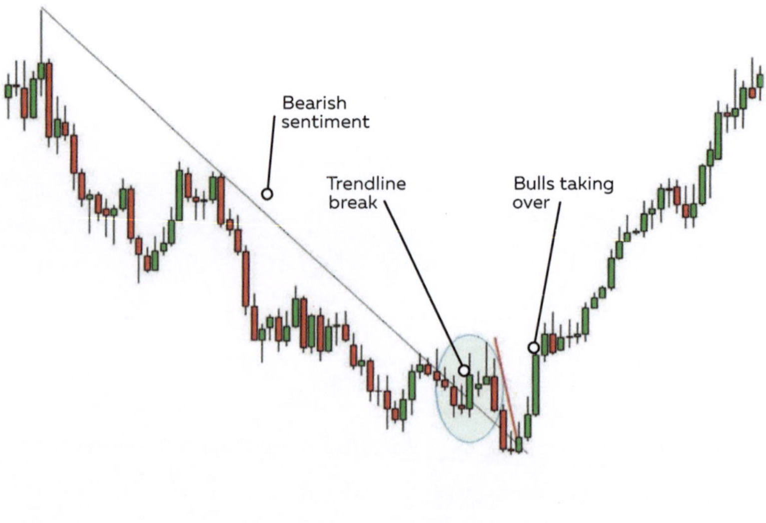

b. Bearish Reversal: a currency pair converts from an uptrend to bearish sentiment.

Reversal patterns can be found in different ways. Remember, we will only explain what works based on the experience we have. It is part of every trader's appeal for technical analysis to have different approaches towards market behavior at key turning points. Here are some descriptive names of reversal patterns:

1.2 Support and Resistance

Support and resistance are effective technical tools, if used properly. They have been used for many years. There are many theories around these tools, but the most important thing is to find something that resonates and works with your personality. We are all in the same market but viewing the price differently.

Every timeframe it is important depending on your style of trading or time you want to be in the market - small timeframe for short-term trades and higher timeframe for a long-term view. Even though many traders overlook a higher timeframe, especially monthly, it is advisable to look at the bigger picture even if you're going to trade on a smaller timeframe, then you need to know where you are in the market. We can't ignore the fact that the higher the timeframe the better.

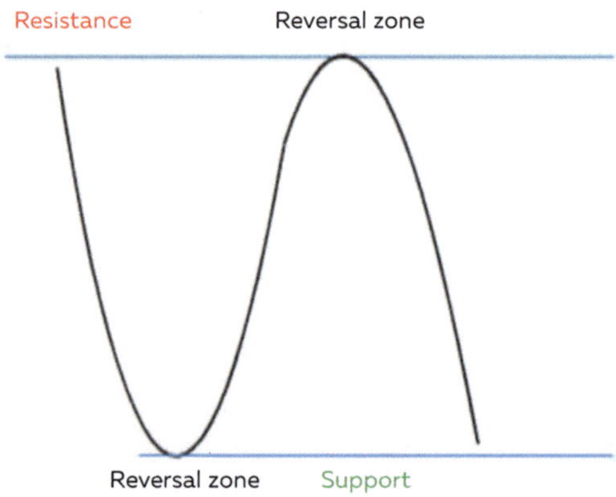

Before the market creates resistance, the market was bullish until it reached a turning point and changed its direction to bearish sentiment. The market can break a support from a bearish sentiment, retest and continuing with its bearish movement.

Same applies with support, an end of bearish sentiment to bullish sentiment or market can break a resistance from bullish sentiment, retest and continue with bearish movement.

The question will always remain at which level can we identify as a potential reversal zone and which will be our support and resistance. The market leaves tracks, which means what happened in the past can possibly happen in the future. Check the picture below.

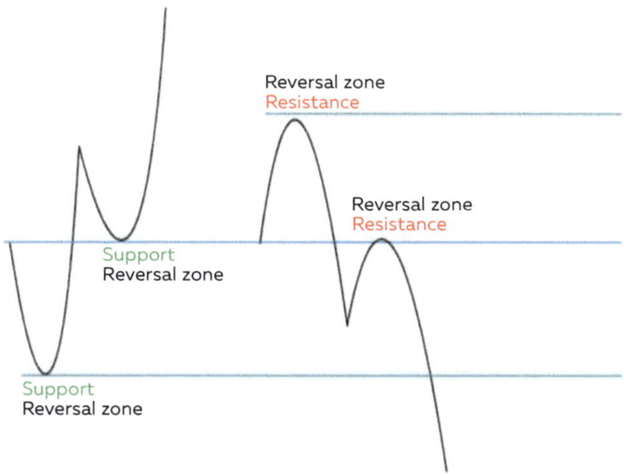

For every candle in the market we have an open, high, low and closing. All represent price, depending on which timeframe you are viewing:

- High of the candle (highest price that the market went)
- Opening of the candle (an opening price before highest price)
- Low of the candle (lowest price the market went)
- Closing (closing price)

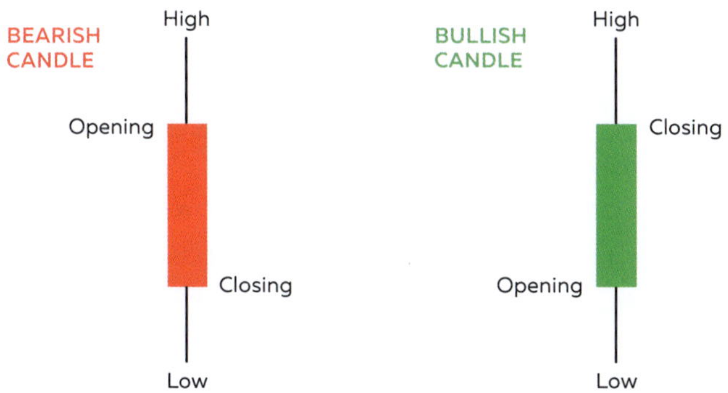

As you can see in the picture below, wicks and opening or closing of the candle are used. The most important levels will always be the last two highest price for resistance and last two lowest price for support.

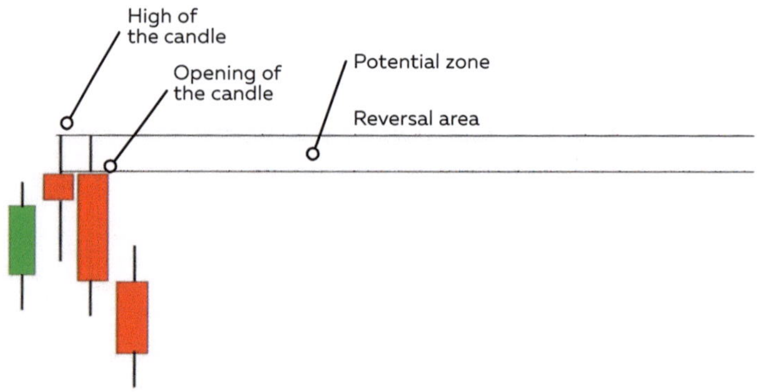

For resistance: You will need to draw your zone on top of the last wick and your second zone will be on opening of the previous bullish candle.

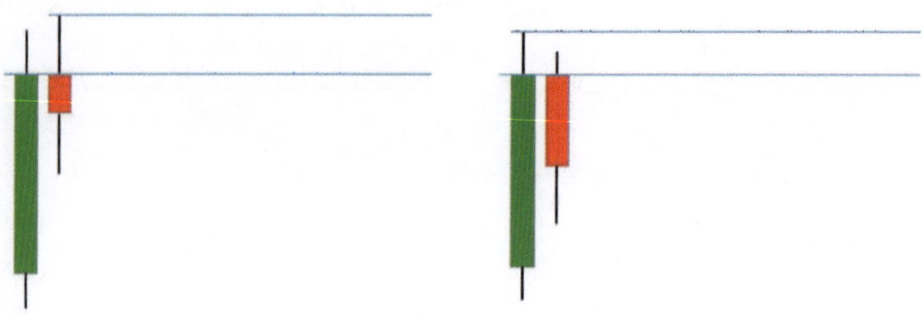

For support: same with the support zone - lowest price which is your last wick and closing price of that previous candle, the main focus here is the last two prices.

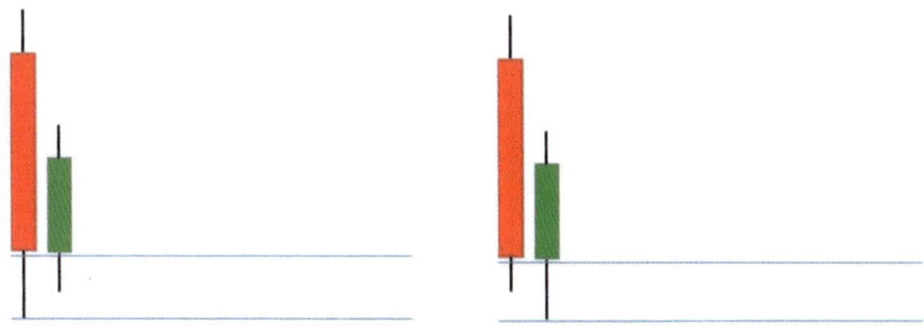

Let us take a look here, the price broke the previous support area. When you go through the book you will learn more and have a clearer understanding of break and retest. In this case, after the price breaks the zone - we're most likely to see a retracement and price retest from the zone it broke - our support was drawn from the low of the wick and the opening.

The basics are, every time price breaks the support, it turns into resistance, and here we see the price retest in that zone that is highlighted from the support area. This is where we are going to look for opportunities in term of selling the market.

Here's another perfect example. Remember you won't always get exactly the same setups as this, but I am pretty sure that every book or any website you've checked or read, show that the patterns don't really come as you saw them in the past.

The goal is to work with your subconscious mind, so you will see these kinds of patterns in the future. The idea is about reading the price and reacting to what the market is giving you.

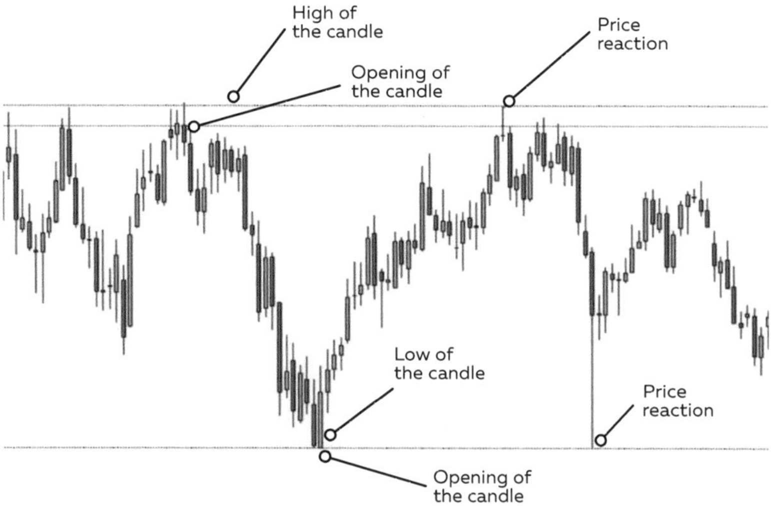

In the above picture we marked our levels off reversal using what we've mentioned. See how the market reacted at these levels of reversal. This is where we are going to look for trades. Sometimes the market will react from your first level or between the levels and leave. It is part of trading, so always wait for what you want from the market, always follow the rules.

1.3 Supply and Demand

Supply and demand trading remains one of the most popular trading strategies. Most people follow other peoples' rules. The reality is that the reason why people trading supply and demand zones are not making consistent profits, is because of the incorrect understanding they have been given about how to find supply and demand zones. In this book, I'll give you the understanding you need to find supply and demand zones that are most likely to give you profitable trades. Find turning points in the price action where prices have reacted sharply. Look at the zone where there is a trendline break, some candles are too big and have big wicks. It is advisable to cover the wick and opening or closing of the candle depending on market sentiment. Examples as follows:

A trendline break

A clean trendline break signifies a good reaction for a supply and demand zone. The cleaner the trendline break, the better the supply and demand zone.

For Demand Zone

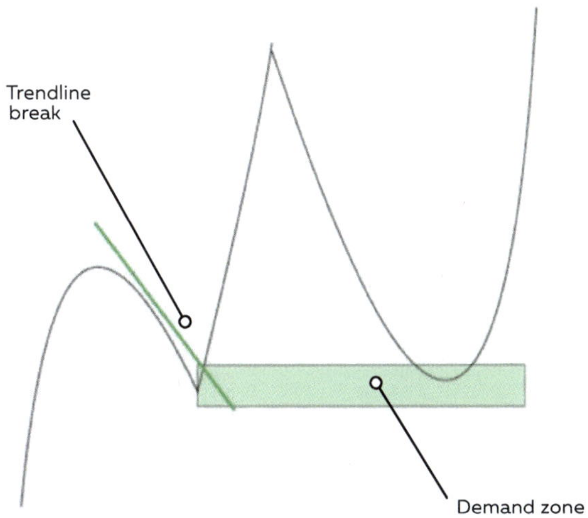

For Supply Zone

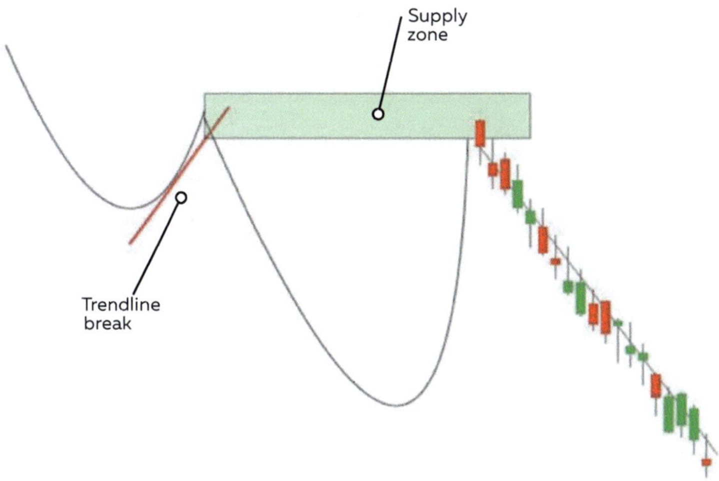

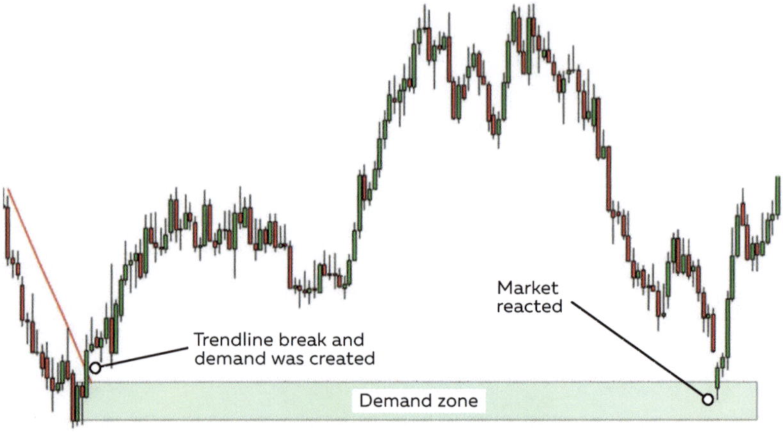

We had a price dip low before the break above and changed the market sentiment to bullish, but the most important thing is how the demand zone was created. A trendline break was the first good sign, and after we've had a trendline break, the question will be which candle must be highlighted?

We need to cover the last candle before the price goes up. Obviously, there are many theories around which candle must be highlighted. We advise you to cover the last candle after the price went up if you are looking for demand zone.

After we followed the rules, price reacted perfectly in that zone for a buy signal.

Sell setup

We had a trendline break and last candle before the market drop was highlighted and price reacted from that zone.

You just have to open your chart and find more examples. We would've included hundreds if not thousands of examples, but we want you to comprehend this teaching as much as possible.

In the following picture, it's a mixture of support and supply and demand method, all detailed in one picture.

If a supply or demand zone is going to cause a reversal after being hit, the market must return to the zone quickly. How quickly it must return is dependent on the timeframe which the supply or demand zone has formed on. For zones on the 1 hour chart the market must return to the zone within 24 hours of it being created. For zones on the daily chart the market must revisit the zone within 30 days after it was created. Note also that the above-mentioned rules are not always the case.

In our experience, we've confused many supply and demand zones that are next to each other. The truth is, sometimes the market can use them both, and that's a whole other story.

There are two supply zones in this scenario. What the price did was to activate the first one, which means there were sellers but it wasn't enough to make a reasonable drop. The price continued to activate the second one before we saw a better drop.

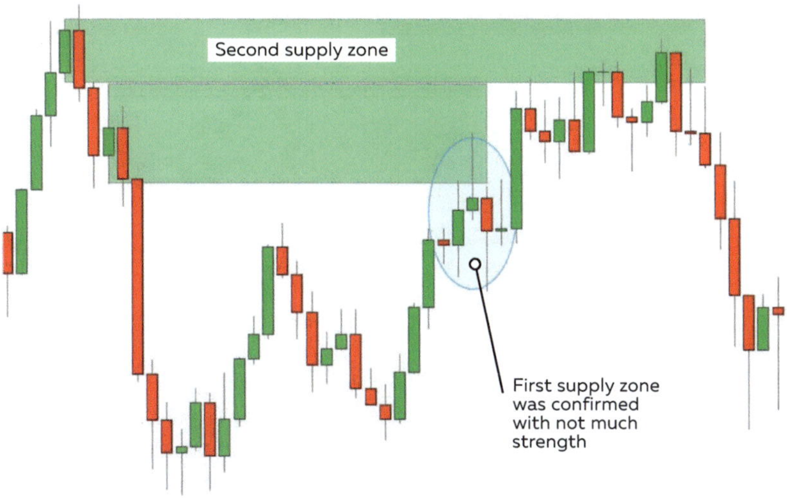

In this second case there are also two supply zones, but the price just used the first one and left.

"DO MORE OF WHAT WORKS AND LESS OF WHAT DOES NOT."

Steve Clark

In conclusion, when you see two supply/demand zones next to each other, trade the first one with caution (risk low as possible) and the second one with a normal risk appetite - we don't mean to risk more but have quality over quantity. Second zones are always preferable.

There are rules for just about everything. Supply and demand have some rules too. Our main goal is to find a reversal zone and watch how the price behaves at that zone so we can act accordingly.

In the picture below, we have a price spiked through a reversal zone. Those spikes don't really disqualify the zone, even though some consider this as a failed zone because other traders will normally put a tight stop loss outside of the zone and get stopped by the market.

This means the price got rejected. As long as the price is still below and respecting the zone we can still wait for proper structure before shorting the market.

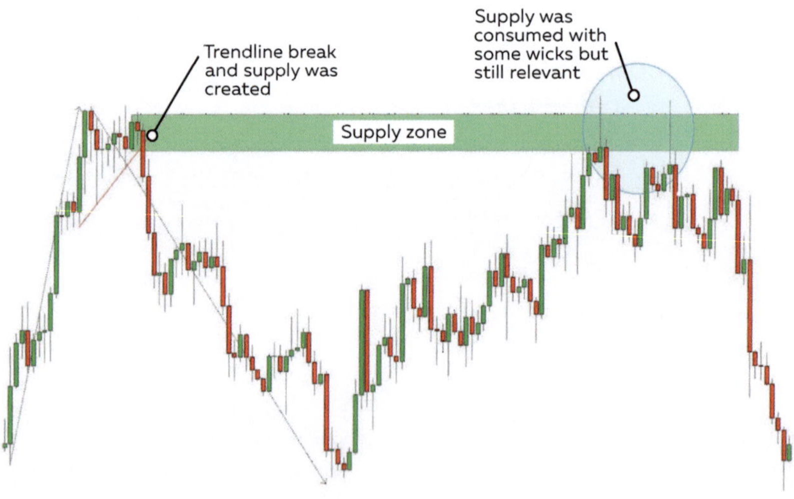

1.4 Trendlines

Trendlines are foremost for technical analyses. A trendline is a line connecting two or more lows, or two or more highs, with the line projected out into future.

For a bullish setup, wait for price to break above before going long. Other traders will jump in right after it broke the trendline, which tends to be dangerous, and is why you will need double confirmations before deciding to take a trade. A break and a counter trendline with a candlestick confirmation.

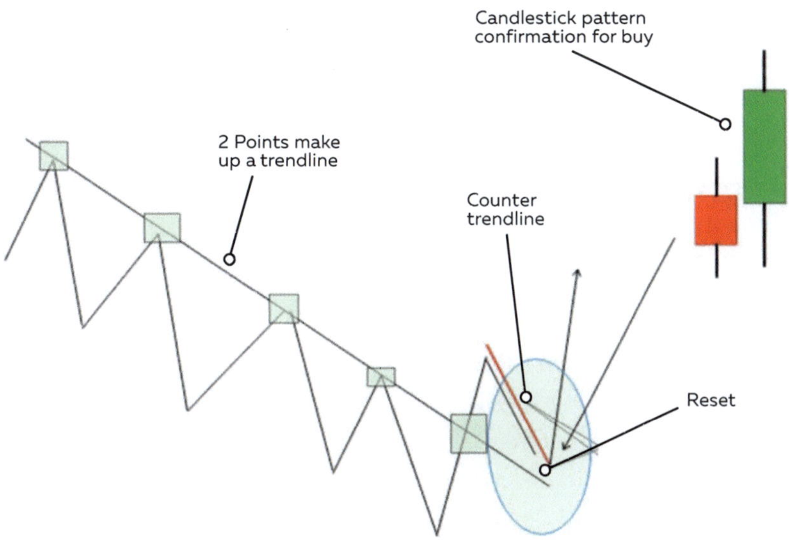

For a Bearish setup, after a price breaks any trendline, wait for retest and draw your trendline for another break before shorting the market.

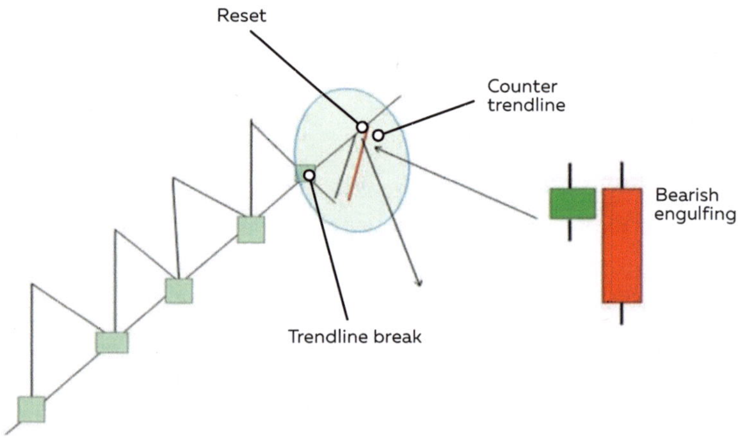

Rules of drawing a Trendline

A trendline must be drawn on top of the wicks. At least two points qualify a trendline, and it's from the third point where we look for potential setups.

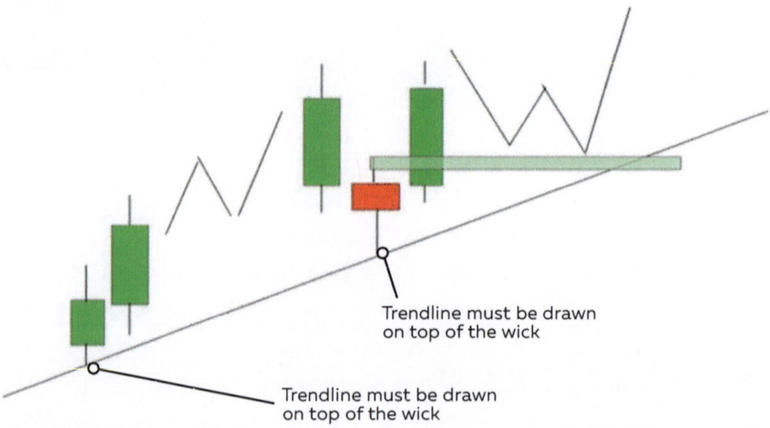

Example:

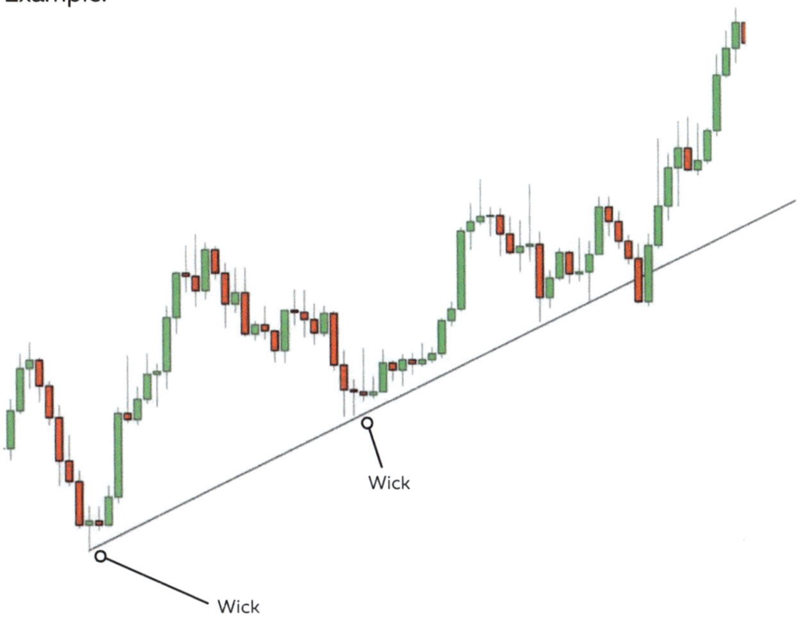

Counter trendline

It's a temporary trendline that is against the actual main trend. It is used to get more confirmation to avoid bad trades and increase accuracy.

Why are counter trendlines so important? They increase high rate of trades, because we all know that sometimes a market can create a false trendline break. To avoid this situation we need at least a break of a trendline and a break of counter trendline. With double confirmations, that allows us to take a trade.

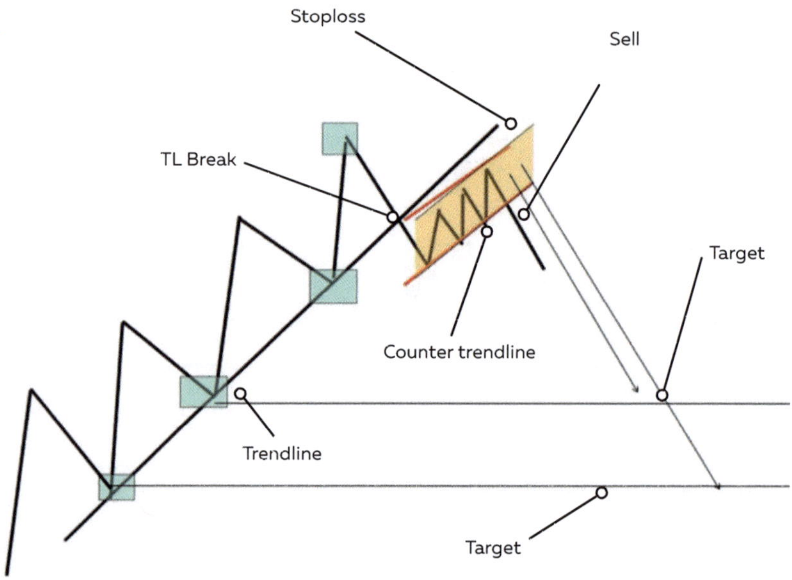

As we know that connecting two or more lows creates a trendline, as shown in the picture above, a clear bullish trendline was created, we had our third touch probably be our buy entry, but the problem started when the price broke that area after we bought. It gives us lots to think about as when the price breaks a trendline we expect a change in market structure. An entry after every break isn't a right way to approach the market, since in this case the market did break but it came back and continued with a bull trendline. After every break you will need at least a counter trendline which will normally confirm a possible change of structure before shorting the market.

The following image is a perfect example of a break, retest and counter trend. A disadvantage of selling after a break is your position can be in a negative for so long before the price resumes,

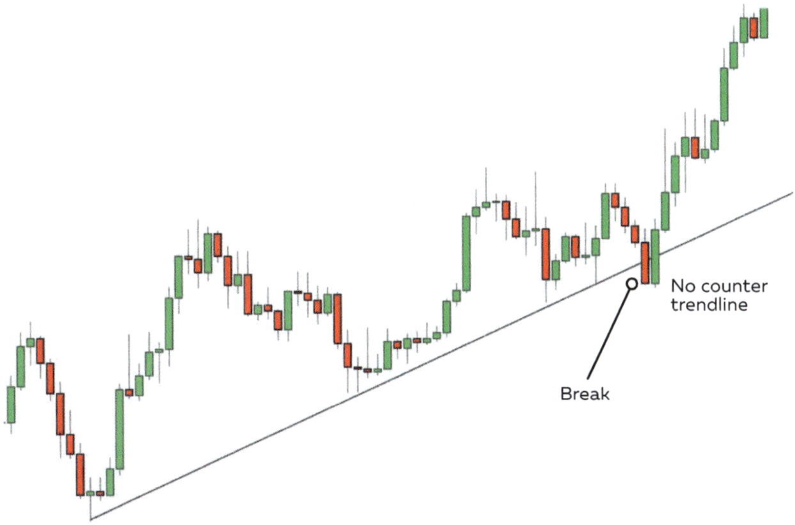

which many traders can't tolerate. Some will usually exit a trade and regret it after the price dropped significantly. Patience will save you from making a lot of bad trades.

Let's analyze the picture. We clearly have a bullish trendline going up, after the price breaks it, a retracement followed to retest it. A counter trendline is drawn using the same principles as a trendline, after a price broke a second trendline, this is where we can take our trades.

Whatever you do in the market, have a concrete reason why you are buying or selling.

Trendlines can be used to gauge market sentiment. Every time the market breaks the trendline, there are chances that the price will revisit the two main points that created the trendline in the first place.

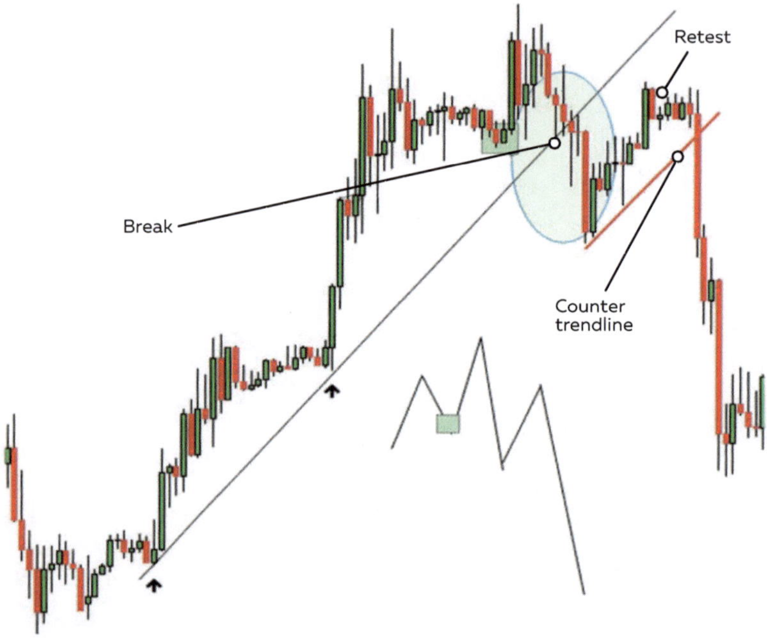

As we know that two or more points creates a trendline, after a break that particular trendline can be still be useful for target purposes. If you have two or more points, you can expect a price to revisit those areas.

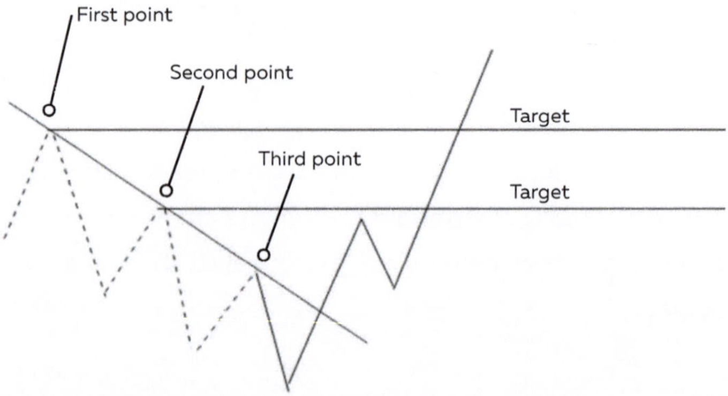

Since we have a trendline that was broken, followed by a retest and a counter trendline, this gives us a good setup to take a position, with trendline points as our future potential target. These can be a minimum level where we can expect the market to go even further.

Trendlines can be powerful if used correctly.

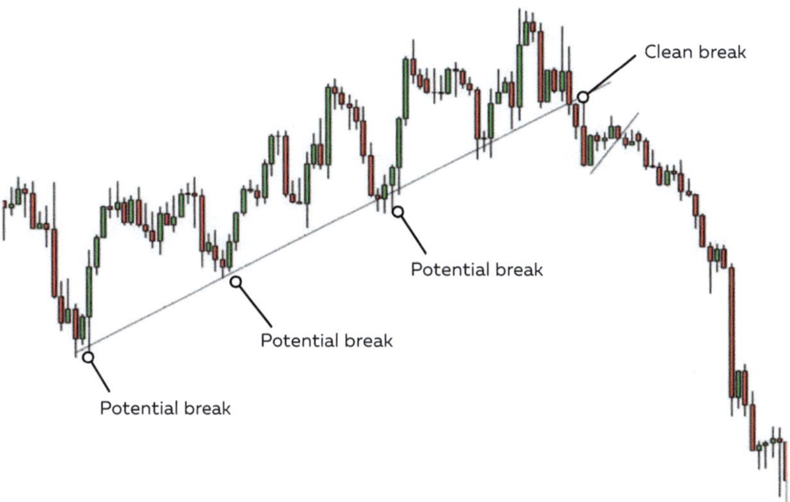

Don't forget the following:

a) Two points make a trendline

b) Draw your line on the pin (wick)

c) For every break of a trend, target the two points that created the trendline.

d) 3rd touch or 3 strike zones is an opportunity to buy/sell.

Trendlines must be drawn on top of the wick.

The Different Types of Trendline

1. Main (First) Trendline

A main trendline can be created over years, held for years and take years to be revisited.

2. Midterm (Second) Trendline

This can be found within a main trendline and can be created over weeks and days.

3. Inner (Third) Trendline

This can be created over days and hours and is mostly found on smaller timeframes.

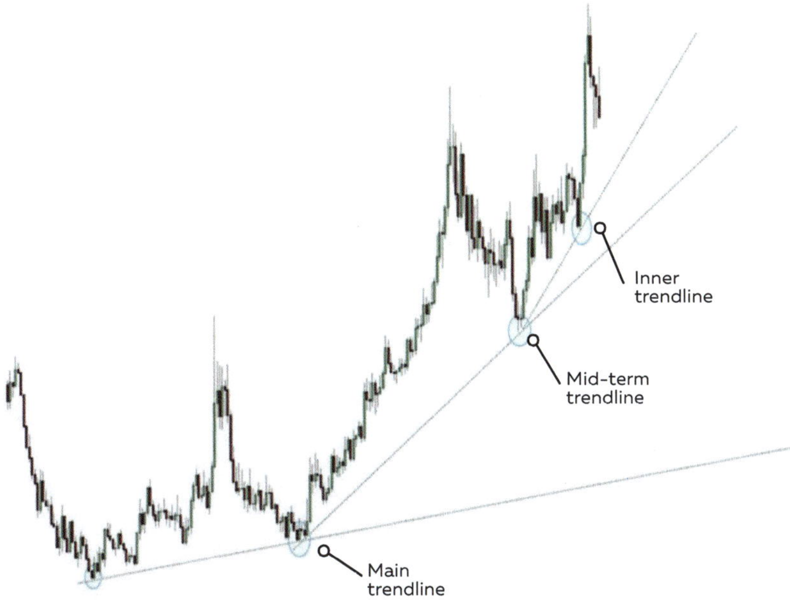

Despite all these, the trendlines are an indication of what the market has been doing and is also trying to project some possible future movement. A trendline can be also be used as an additional tool for your trading system.

Highs and Lows

We all know that these are among the basic things in the market, but we thought we should clarify some other things. Mostly called Higher highs/Higher lows and Lower lows/Lower highs depending on the direction of the market (market sentiment), but to crush all this confusion, we normally call them highs and lows. Every time price breaks support and resistance, a new high/low will probably form, waiting for a price to retest before forming that low.

There are three things that you need to consider when trading lows and highs in the market.

a) A clean break at critical zone (support and resistance or supply and demand)
b) A shallow retracement to the previous broken zone
c) Where is the next major reversal zone? (Potential target)

A bullish setup

In a series of highs and lows, we are focusing on the new highs, also considering a clean break, and remember every time the market creates a new high, a possible high will follow.

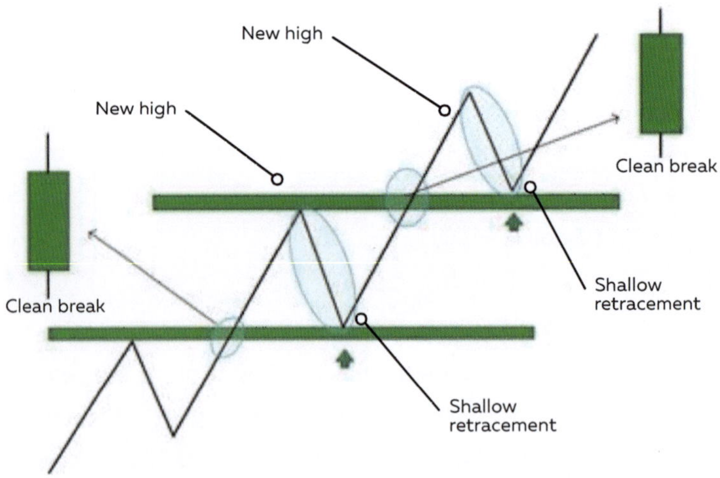

A bearish sentiment

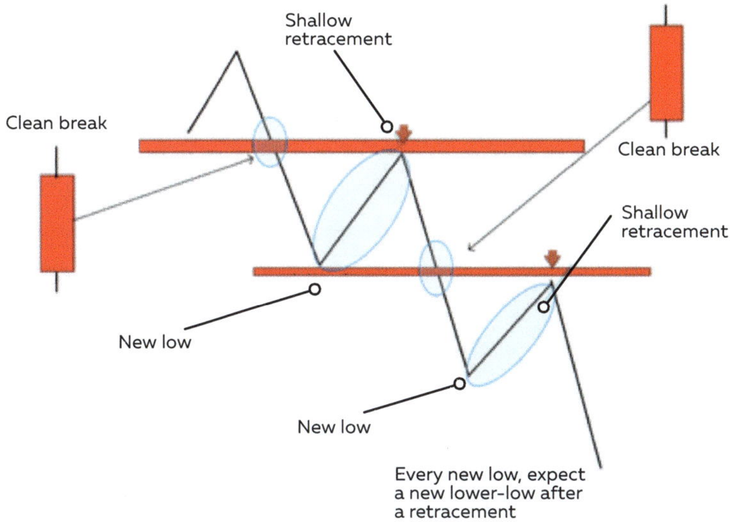

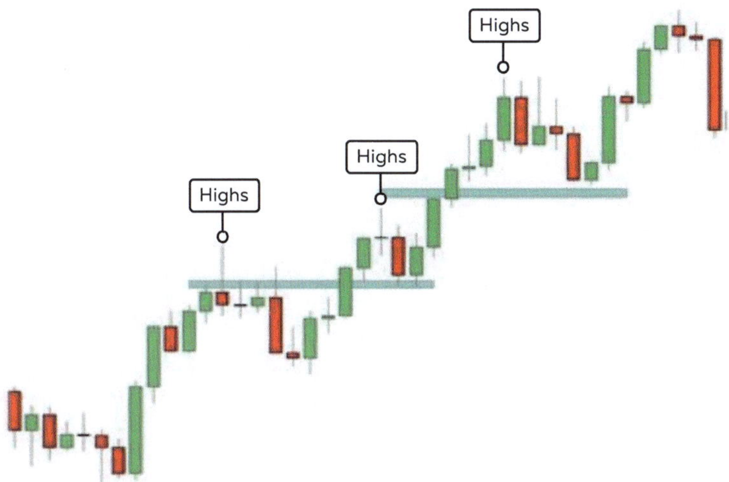

THE WAY PRICE BREAKS THE RESISTANCE COUNTS A LOT

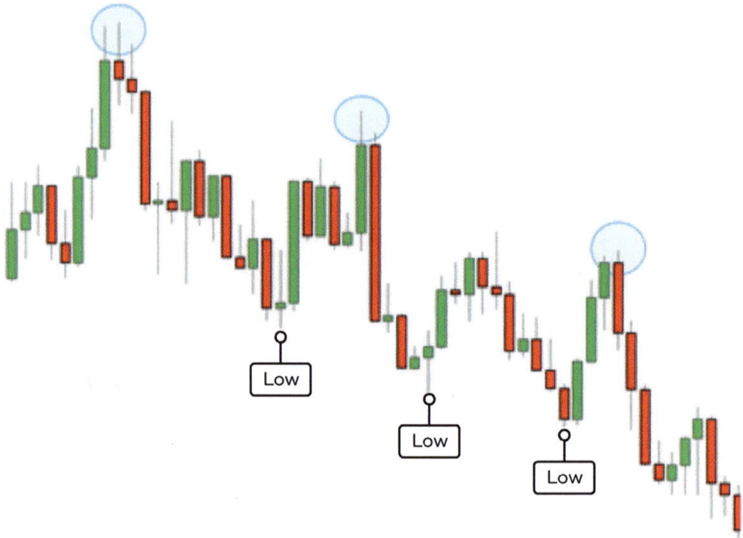

BASIC BUY SETUP OF HIGH AND LOW:

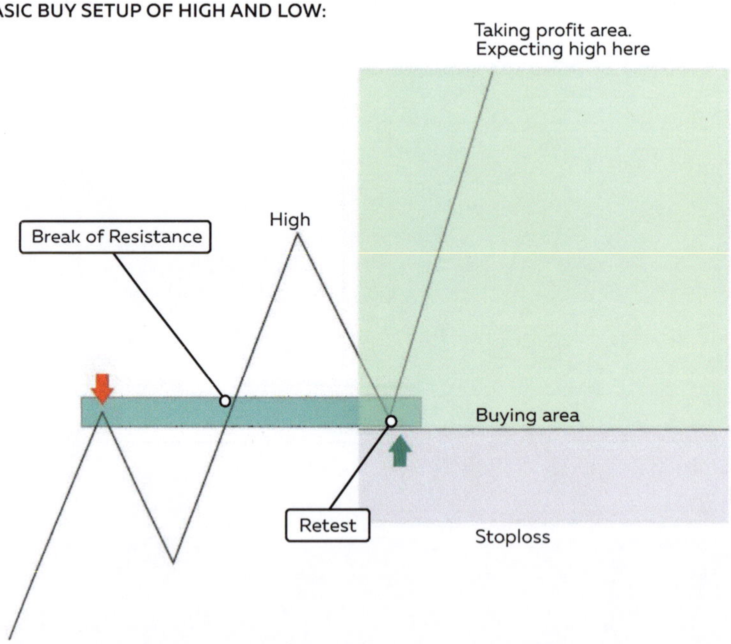

The price will normally break resistance and turn into support. You have to consider the behavior of how the price broke that level of resistance. A clear break shows some strength in the market, a sign that more buyers are in the market. You don't want to see yourself trading against the sentiment. After the price created a new high, the price retrace and retest in that level it broke (support), this is where we buy expecting another high as our target.

BASIC SELL SETUP OF HIGH AND LOW:

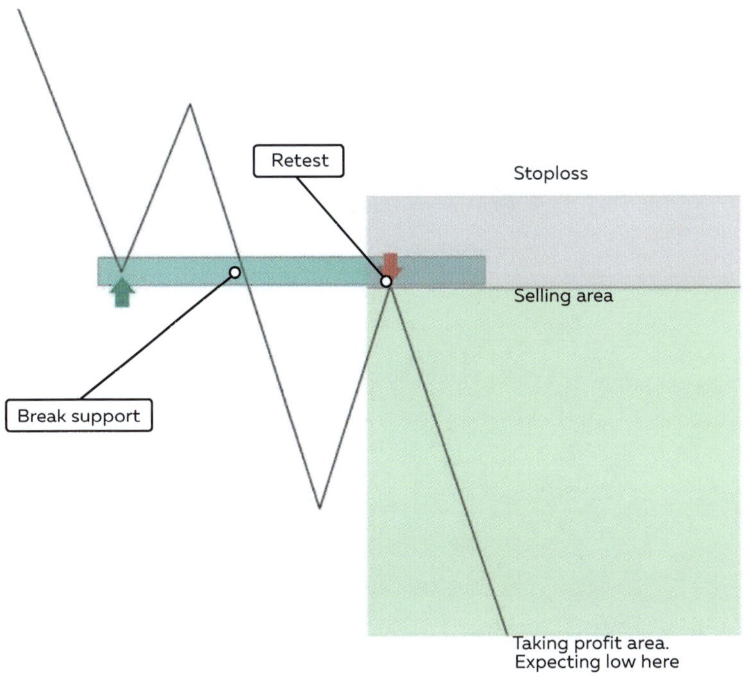

Sometimes we complicate things by looking at things that are not even there. We just have to react on what we've been given, because if we don't follow the rules and take from the market, that means we are going to give something to the market.

2.

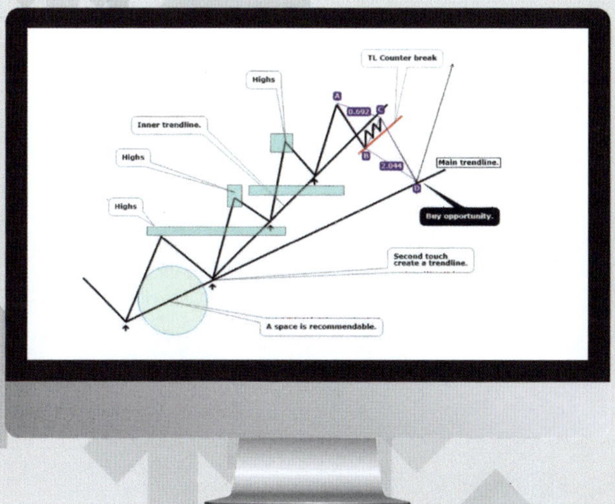

CANDLE BEHAVIOUR

We've studied candlesticks and their names. Admittedly keeping up with up with names was not our strong suit, but we kept watching how the price moved. It's how we realised that understanding price is king and the way candles move says a lot about the state of the market.

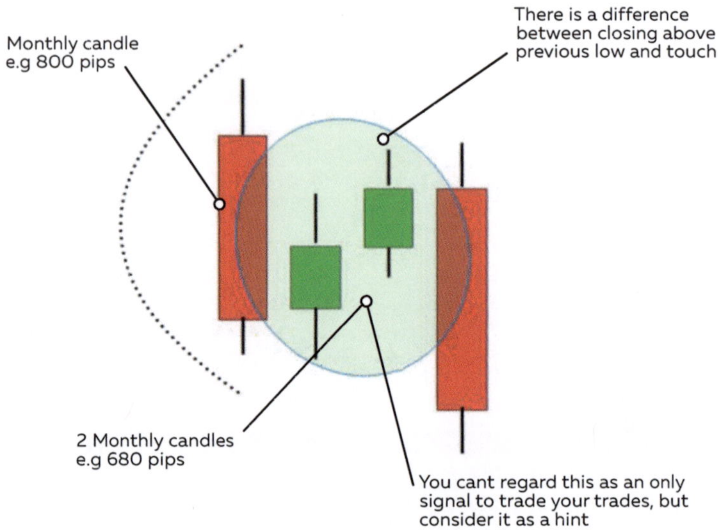

It took one month to generate approximately 800pips while two monthly candles generate about 680pips. This indicates that it is easier to find sellers than buyers. Why retracement always takes more time than the actual move?

2.1 Institutions

Closing trades and taking profits can only be achieved when there are enough orders present in the market. If a bank has a big sell position placed, the only way they're going to be able to take profits off the sell position is if other traders come into the market and place buy trades. They will try to convince traders to buy their positions that they consider as taking profit, after that they load more to that direction.

Psychological retracements take time and frustrate many trades, this is because many traders don't have patience to wait. They want to see themselves in the market every tick of a price and end up missing a big move. A high timeframe is king.

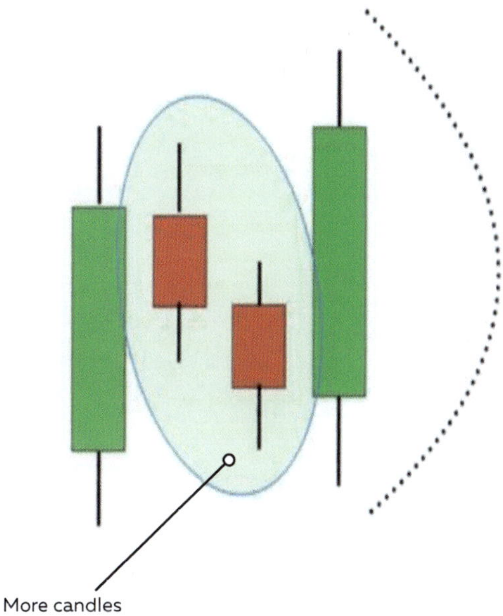

You will see the price push the market aggressively or more pips moving in a certain direction with one big candle but fail to cover the same number of pips on the opposite with more candles.

A high timeframe is good for projecting long term trade. Since we've mentioned that retracements are shallow in nature, lacking volume because of profit taking. If you open your chart and check every timeframe you will see this structure everywhere. Price will drop without any disruption and retrace slowly before the drop.

Bullish sentiment retracement

We have five candles in the following picture - two of them are bullish and three are bearish candles. We have one big bullish candle going up, followed by three bearish candles going down. The big question remains, why the three candles failed to cover one candle on the opposite side?

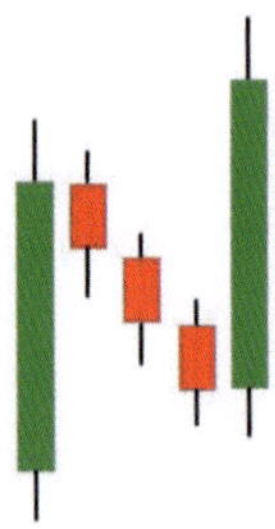

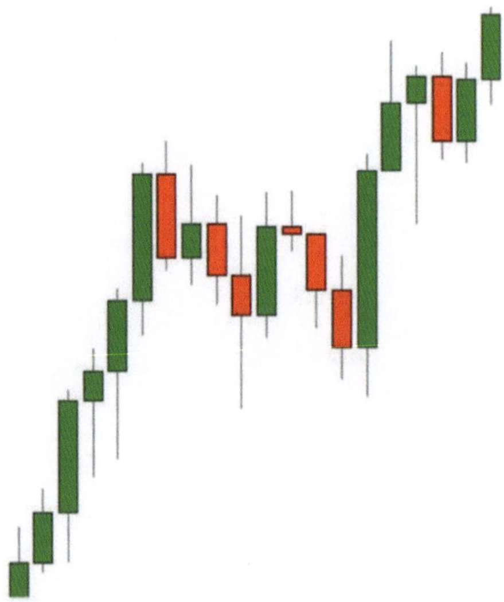

When the market is strongly bullish, big bullish and small bearish candles will be seen.

Bearish market retracement

When the market pushes price down, more big bearish candles will be seen than big bullish candles. There is one big bearish candle followed by a bullish candle which serves as a retracement and shows that there are few buyers in the market.

Sometimes you will see a quick retracement but it should not bother you, because of understanding the big picture, know where you are at. Bearish market with a quick retracement.

2.1 How a monthly candle is formed

There are basics but many people are still confused about the importance of a higher timeframe. Smaller timeframes are for entries and scalping, but you can't do your analyses on these timeframes and expect to see a bigger picture. A monthly candle is made up of 4 weekly candles, while weekly candles include five daily candles. What normally happens is that at the beginning of the month (in the first week of 4), if market sentiment is bullish, it will normally open on the opposite side of the trend before resuming to market sentiment. That is why most monthly candles have wicks.

The first week of the month may possibly be the high/low of the month although the opposite may apply and other weeks start to follow an actual market trend. In the same way a weekly candle may have a same scenario as a monthly candle, the first few days of the week can be misleading - Monday, Tuesday and sometimes even Wednesday create a possible high/low of the week and a

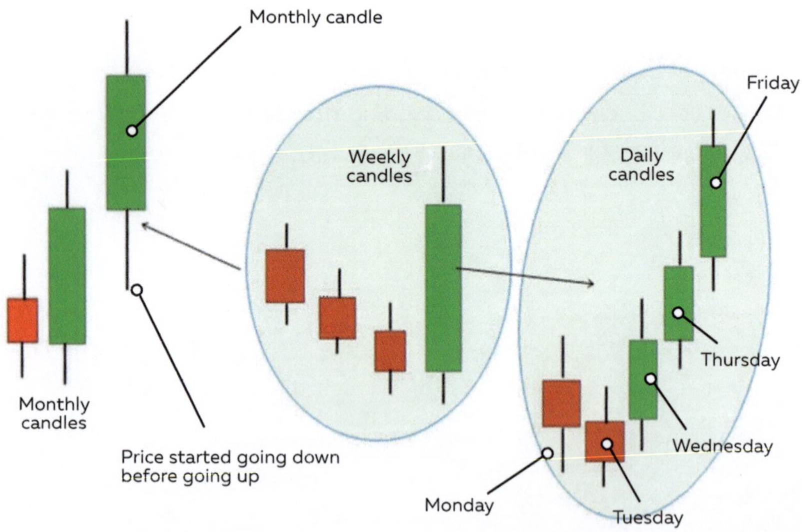

high/low of that month. Viewing the market on the higher timeframe will help you a lot with the understanding of market direction and making better decisions on the smaller timeframes.

Daily

Daily candles are created by 3 sessions - Asian, London and US.
Asian session: It ranges in most cases unless you trade commodities currencies (NZD & AUD). JPY also move at that time and most NZD, AUD & JPY news are released at that time.
London session: European opening
US session

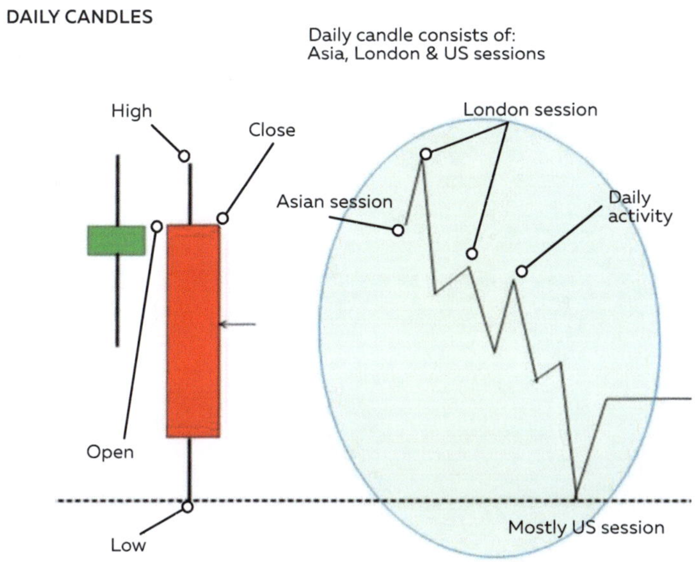

We don't normally look at sessions that much as sessions mean more money coming in, as volatility increase. Patterns and understanding the market sentiment is what we want to look for in the market.

3.

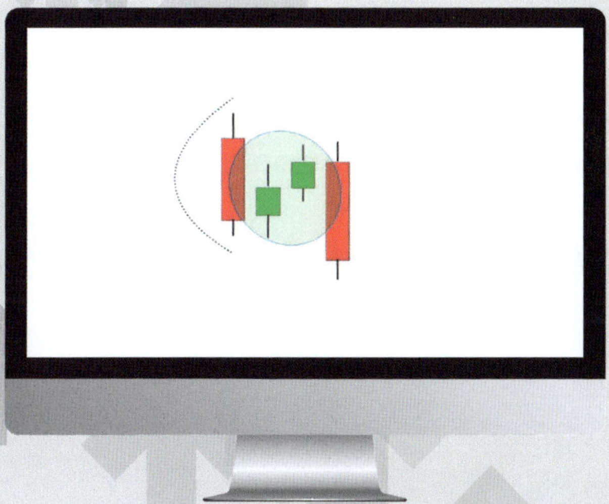

FADE OF MOMENTUM

Reading price momentum

Momentum in the market signifies a lot of behaviors such as gain or loss of strength. The most important thing in the market is to read the state of the market condition. Hope and belief don't work- as traders you need to trade based on what you see not what you think. The goal of trading is to project and anticipate.

The two types of momentum:

a) Fade of momentum (bulls/bears)
b) Gain of momentum (bulls/bears)

Fade of momentum (bears) and Gain of momentum (bears)
Fade of momentum can appear everywhere, which is why it is advisable to use it at the reversal areas. These are examples of momentum:

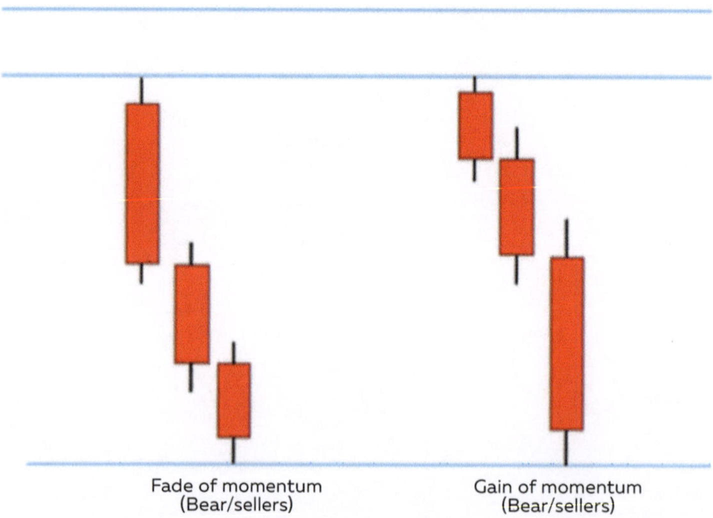

Fade of momentum (bulls) and Gain of momentum (bulls)

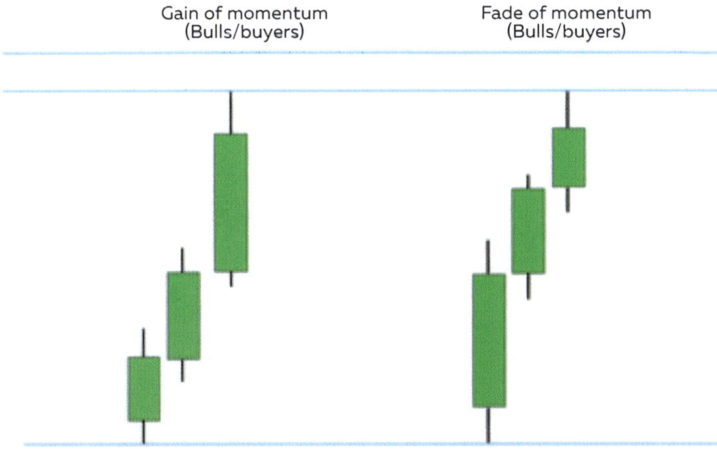

For example, in this picture below, we see a gain of momentum from our reversal zone (support). It shows that buyers came in - for future reference we are expecting almost the same when price leaves that level. Focusing on fading of bearish momentum, there was a momentum going down but when the price approached our reversal zone, candles started to lose momentum and buyers came in, which is where buyers are expected to come in.

(Note that we already mention different patterns that are found around reversal zone). Price left the support by gaining momentum, then followed by shallow retracement (profit taking), it continued before it dropped and the supply zone was set.

Bullish fading

Watch how the price behaves when it approaches the supply zone, we see a drop (a shallow retracement) (profit taking) and price resumes with bearish movement.

Fading of buyer's momentum

Price lost bullish momentum and gained bearish momentum. A 1-5 structure presented itself with a small retracement before it dropped again.

Fading of seller's momentum

If you can look at the previous picture, you can tell that these behaviors on the following picture are the same. Price dropped before rising. Look at the last four candles before the price changed direction. We have a big bearish candle followed by a small one before the two other candles (who were already fading and on the hand) price started to change direction and bull candles started to gain strength with the price going up.

The most important thing is finding an ideal reversal zone and watching these kind of behaviors.

4.

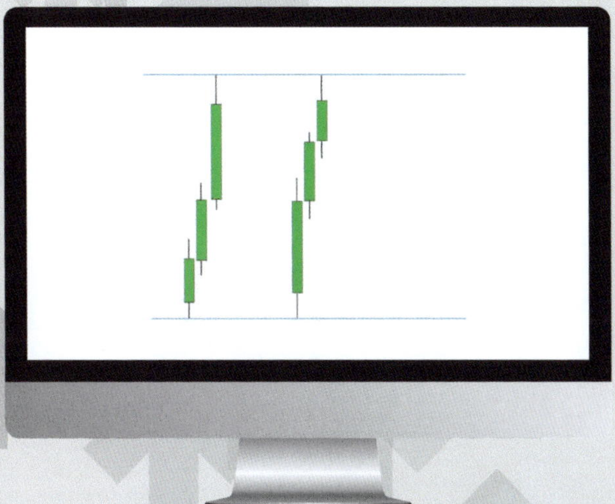

MONTHLY HIGH & LOW

Candle closing is important when it comes to market direction. First thing we need to look at is previous high and low closings, as this is what determines the sentiment of the market. If monthly candles are breaking the low but never break the high, bearish sentiment is set, same applies to bullish market.

Remember there isn't only one tool to take any trade. There are other things that we should consider first.

When you look at the last downtrend you will notice that the price had been going down for months. It took almost 12 months before the price came close to previous month highs.

The sentiment was bearish all along. In other timeframes, there were many signals for buy and sell. More than likely, there were traders who were looking for reversal and got burned as the sign of reversal wasn't even there.

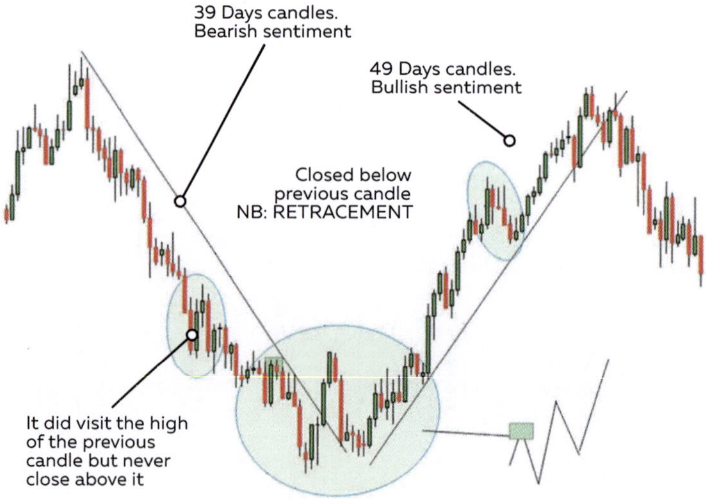

In terms of holding and swinging the market

As long as the price is breaking the highs of the previous month, bullish is set, same goes when the market is breaking lows, the bearish is set. Let's analyse this pair (monthly timeframe) from 1 July 2008 to 1 August 2012, about 4 years of activity.

Firstly there are three bearish candles that show a momentum that bears are in control. Out of 11 months of drop, we see the first retracement where bullish close above previous monthly highs. But the following candles lost momentum and started showing signs that bullish was taking over. The price continued for another 16 months (489 days) without closing above the previous month highs.

Out of 48 months of monthly candles, price only closed three times above previous months, it was only a retracement. This is a 4 year bearish market.

Here is another example from 2012 to 2018

At the end of 2012 the market started to be bullish for about two and a half years, and out of those 29 months price only broke the low of the previous month. This meant that from 2012 till the end of 2014 the price was bullish. Think about the traders who tried to draw a more bearish line to short the market on a smaller timeframe and the market didn't even bother, it just kept on going up.

After the end of a bullish market, we see a change of structure, a big bearish candle closing below four monthly candles. After four candles (4 months) of dropping, the price retraced about 3 candles (3 months) before resuming again.

Out of 18 months (548 days) the price only closed once above the previous month. Between the beginning of 2015 and the end of 2016, the market was bearish and only favoured bearish sell patterns.

The price can drop in early February and retrace in March, April and May before resuming (continuation) in June. The reason this occurred was that the market range was more than it's trend. (Trend for 2 months and retrace for more than 3 months or so).

Most of the strategies, indicators, and EAs work in the market but the question is where and when? Remember we spoke about the market that can trend for around 2 months and retrace for around 4 months.

Here is a trick... You can create a system that is psychologically based only on the trending market, obviously it will work for a couple of months before it starts taking the money back to the market.

Let us look at the picture below. We are looking at 24 months of trading - price went up then retraced before a major continuation. Price was busy with the highs of previous months which confirmed a bullish sentiment.

"WIN OR LOSE, EVERYBODY GETS WHAT THEY WANT FROM THE MARKET. SOME PEOPLE SEEM TO LIKE TO LOSE, SO THEY WIN BY LOSING MONEY."

Ed Seykota

On another timeframe, there is a beautiful continuation pattern that played out pretty well (Textbook pattern). Now you can see why we say every system out there works but you must know where and when to use them.

Above is a daily timeframe. Almost 22 days of trading, the bullish sentiment was set - even though the market was closing below yesterday's low it wasn't convincing as all the retracements where shallow.

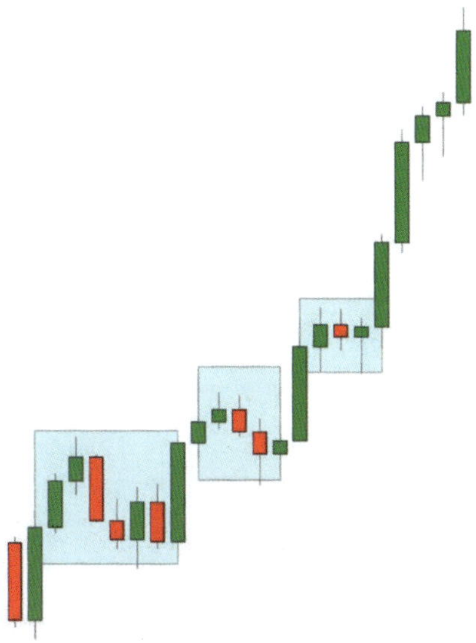

This setup is worth discussing (a rally retrace rally).

Monthly, weekly and daily lows are important because they signify how the market closes at the end of the month, week and day. It's based on a daily timeframe but can be applied to both monthly and weekly timeframes - the concept is the same. Remember you can find a structure on a one-minute timeframe as well as a monthly timeframe, the differences will be time.

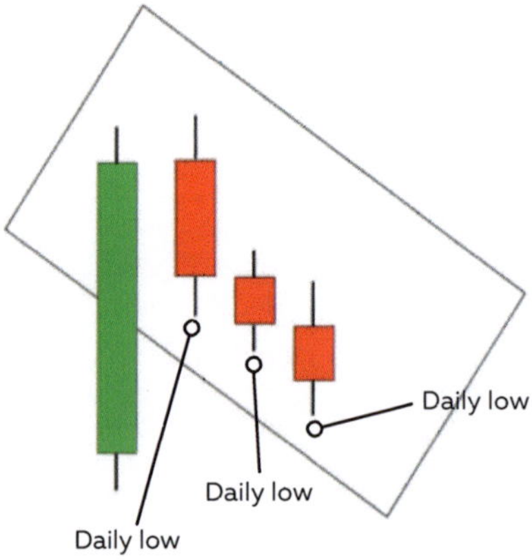

Breaking of previous lows and struggling to break the previous high of the candle remains an important tool to consider when reading the price. When price trends down it will rarely break previous daily highs clearly, because the bearish will be in control.

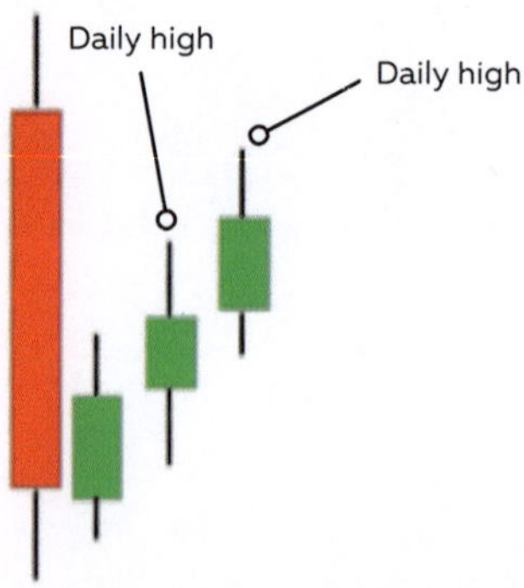

This is a structure you find when the market is retracing bullish structure. These are building structures for a buy and sell setup.

Sell setup build up structure:

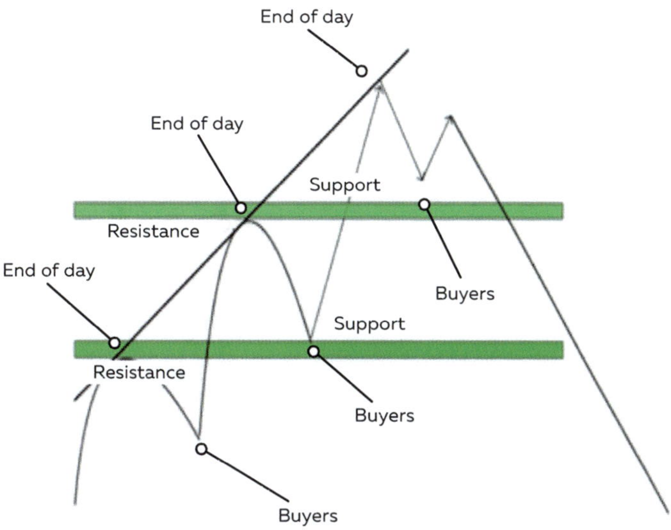

Buy setup build up structure:

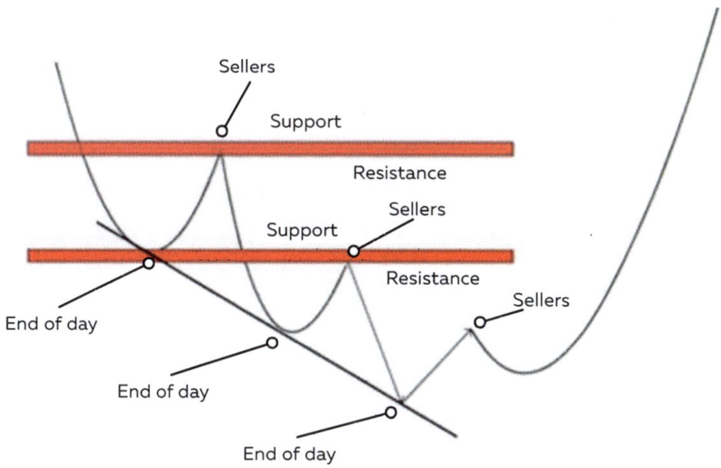

A build up structure in detail:

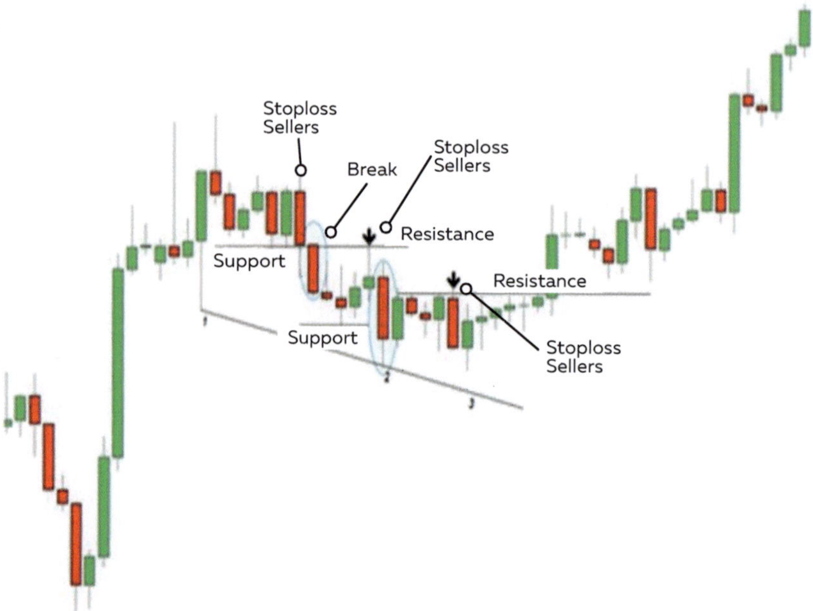

After the price rallies up, most traders will expect a continuation, which eventually will happen but not as quickly as they wish. We did mention that banks don't trade like us - before they enter any trade they have to create a space for them to come in, which is liquidity, it's all about money - when you look at the charts, smart money sees money on the other side.

Many times we're in a trade for hours or a day without seeing profit or merely seeing small profit. Remember the market just takes one candle to correct all the accumulation. We've all been there, there, this is the reason you need to understand the nature of retracement.

There is a series of support and resistance being broken and retested. On a smaller timeframe you will think the trend is changing, more people will start to sell against the trend. The more people who are convinced that the trend has changed or the more sell setups/ signals are legit the more liquidity is provided. On the other hand, the more the orders, the more money in the market. This can be done in every timeframe. Other accumulations take months, weeks, days, hours and minutes and is the reason you need patience more than anything in this business.

In this scenario, the market dropped more than three times to convince traders who are afraid to sell at the first drop after a rally. Many people who are not convinced because they are still thinking about confirmation, will probably get burnt buy the second drop. This is where traders are starting to be convinced that the market is changing the trend and they will be ready at the third structure. Unfortunately the third structure near reversal can be suicidal because this is where we find 123 confluences with a reversal zone. We can have 4 structures but the most important ones are the last 3 before the reversal zone.

Strong previous low close

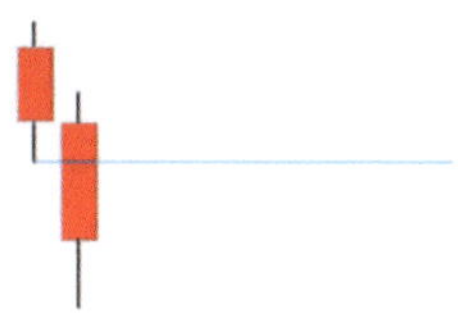

Weak previous low close

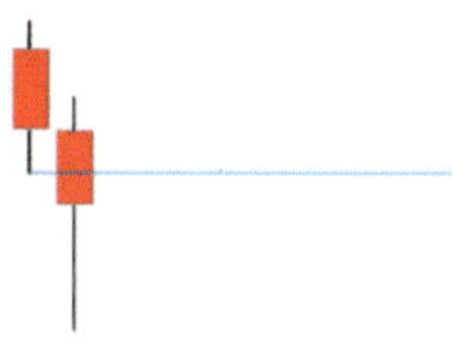

Strong previous high close

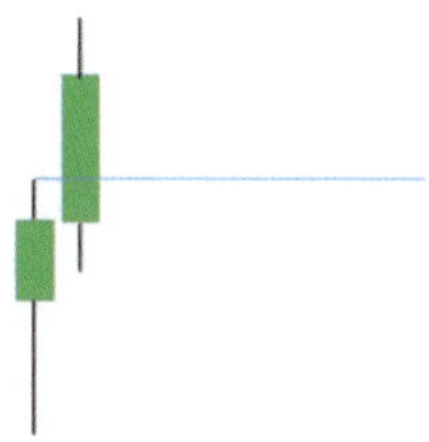

Weak previous high close

Strong previous low closing shows that there are more sellers trying to come in the market. Weak previous low closing shows less interest from bears (sellers), as you can expect more bullish sentiment coming soon. The above also applies for bullish patterns, where strong previous high closing shows that there are more buyers trying to come into the market. Weak previous high closing shows that buyers are losing interest in the price and a sell might be coming soon.

Remember this is not a strategy but some of the aspects that you will need to consider when you are reading the price.

Since everything is governed by law and order, so is the market. We all know that the market is often driven by fear and greed, everyone wants to make more money. Universal laws govern human beings and human nature governs the market. There's a system that governs human beings that lead to certain human behaviours. This is the reason many patterns and other events reoccur over time.

From a one minute to a monthly timeframe, all structures are the same. It might be hard for someone who is not that familiar with the market charts, but the more you look at charts or the longer you've been trading, you will realise that the following charts (structure) are the same.

The following pictures shows this repetitive structure and behavior. Not all traders are the same, some prefer certain timeframes due to personal preferences, but if you want to hold or swing the market, you will need to look at 15 minutes or daily timeframes the same as weekly or monthly timeframes.

In the end it is all about patience, and you will see the reoccurrence of the same patterns.

1 Minute

4 Hour

1 Hour

Weekly

5.

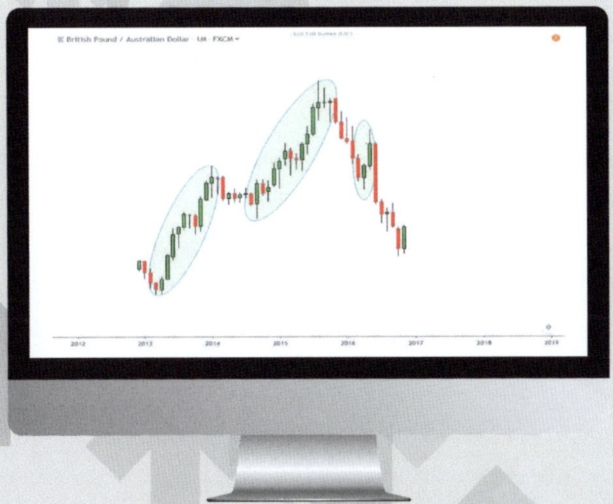

DIVERGENT & 123 MARKET STRUCTURE

What is Divergent?

We can safely say most indicators are lagging, because they record the price as it plays out. When the price moves up or down the indicator normally does the same, but that doesn't stop us from using them when it comes to divergent as we normally see the price go down and the indicator changes its direction to the opposite.

There are many indicators that can be used to spot divergent. In our experience RSI is the best, that is why are using it and will continue using it throughout this book.

Bullish Divergent for Bullish Setup

Looking at the picture we have a 123 structure, but in this case we're going to be looking at the divergent. The first (1) price recorded the move as the indicator followed, same as the second (2) move but now the indicator stopped following the third (3) drop which gave a divergence, which behaves normally to give us a sign that a potential reversal is coming.

Bearish Divergent for Sell Setup

Price kept going up from 1 and 2 as recorded by RSI but 3 was equal on the RSI while on the chart 3 went above 2. Even though price is equal on the RSI but not equal on the chart, we can still consider it as a divergent, as long 3 doesn't go beyond 2.

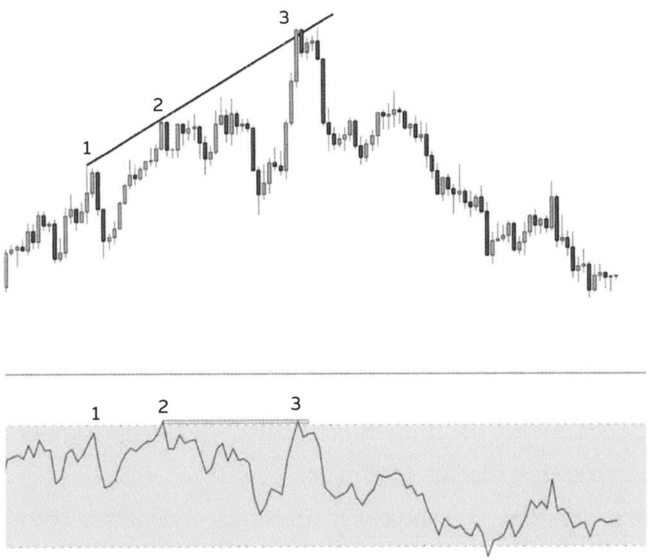

We understand that most of the indicators are lagging, they are not in the present and always behind the market because they are driven by price and price always moves first. So how on earth are they supposed to tell us what's going to happen in the future? Obviously, they can't, they won't and never will. I remember being told that we must stop wasting our time and put the indicators in the bin – which is exactly why I went back to these indicators and used them. The sentiment of getting rid of the indicators is half true if you are going to use them incorrectly for signal purposes only.

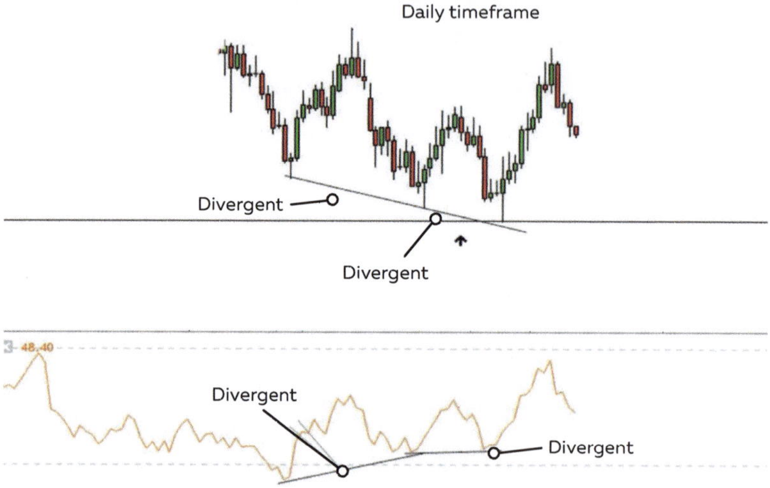

Look at the price 1 and 2, then check the indicator, but level 3 is telling us a different story. The indicator stopped following the price or recorded negatively. This is what we call a divergence. A divergence will be used most often at the reversal zone or at the end of a trend or market sentiment.

Price dips and the indicator followed – same for the second move -but failed to record the third move which was supposed to go below the previous low of 2.

A trendline break can be regarded as another sign as we mentioned early, every time price breaks the trendline there's potential of a retest before price levels, this applies on RSI.

Here is another example of the above, which will make more sense after you've completed the 123 market structure behavior pattern. Level 2 and 3 are important because they happen at the reversal zone.

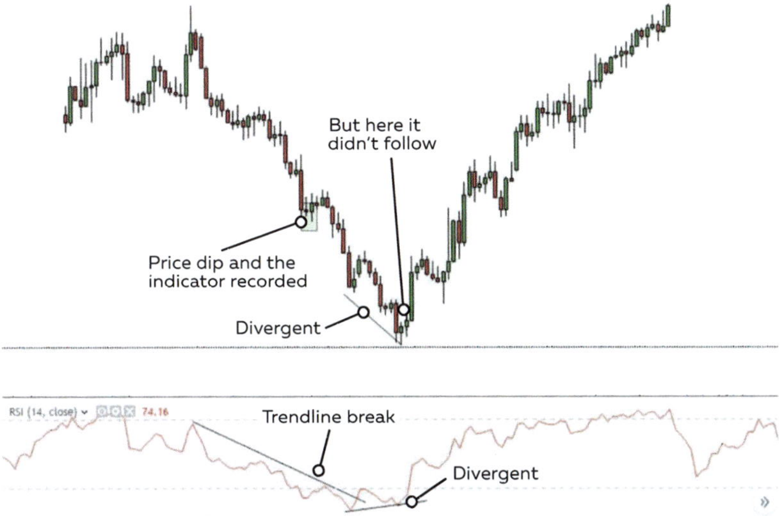

Every indicator is useful depending on how an individual trader is using it.

"IF YOU CAN LEARN TO CREATE A STATE OF MIND THAT IS NOT AFFECTED BY THE MARKET'S BEHAVIOUR, THE STRUGGLE WILL CEASE TO EXIST."

Mark Douglas

5. The 123 Market Behavior Pattern

This pattern gives a good indication of market behavior and also signals if the trend will be changing direction. We previously explained the different types of reversal zones that must be taken into consideration. The 123 structure or market behavior is the pattern that the market usually follows when it is about to reverse its condition.

Remember you need to identify the reversal zone, because if you can't, you can't trade 123 structures.

Try to do some sort of top-down analysis. This involves looking at the bigger picture first and then analysing the details of smaller components. Before we can dive into 123 structures, I will run through our previous explanation.

You have to identify the reversal zones through learning. We've provided, support and resistance, supply and demand and trend line methods.

Step 1:

Find a reversal zone.

Step 2:

Look for a potential divergent on the next timeframe.

The reason we are looking for a divergent is simply to get more confirmation for reversal and entries. A higher timeframe divergent will have a high rate of working out.

The highlighted part above is something that has already happened. Once you see the indicator stop following the price like it should be, switch timeframe and look for another divergent inside the divergent that is building up.

Step 3:

This is what I call 123 structure, it appears almost everywhere since the market moves in waves, but you might not know which wave to trade. For us, when it appears next to the reversal zone, there are criteria that we look for and some we've mentioned already.

When you switch to other timeframe, you are going to see the exact structure which indicates a 123 structure with a divergence within a divergent that's building up on daily timeframe.

Hopefully you now get the whole picture of this method. Let's recap again before doing more examples of entries, stop loss and target. Here is the checklist:

a) Reversal Zone (Support and resistance, supply and demand and trend line)
b) Divergent. (Daily in most cases)
c) Highlight second leg of the divergent.
d) Look for 123 structure with 4-hour timeframe.
e) RSI break and retest. (To be explained)

Remember 123 structure can be identified as 3 wave structures where 2 and 3 can give us another divergent despite the one that the daily timeframe gave us. Check RSI and draw a counter trendline between 2 and 3 waves high or low.

5.1 Entry Point, Stop Loss and Target

- **Entry Point:** The price will break the RSI trendline with the indicator and retest it as a divergent and trendline break.
- **Stop Loss:** This should always be below the reversal area adding spread.
- **Target:** Remember every time the trendline breaks, the price revisits the points that created the trendline.

The most important thing is to find the ideal reversal zone and use this method to enter your trades. This will help you avoid bad trades, and while it doesn't mean you'll always win, it does increase your success rate.

5.2 Reversal Tendency

The market is all about behaviors and as traders we react on what they're giving us, so every action has a corresponding reaction, even the little things matter. In the following diagram there are behaviors that we will discuss.

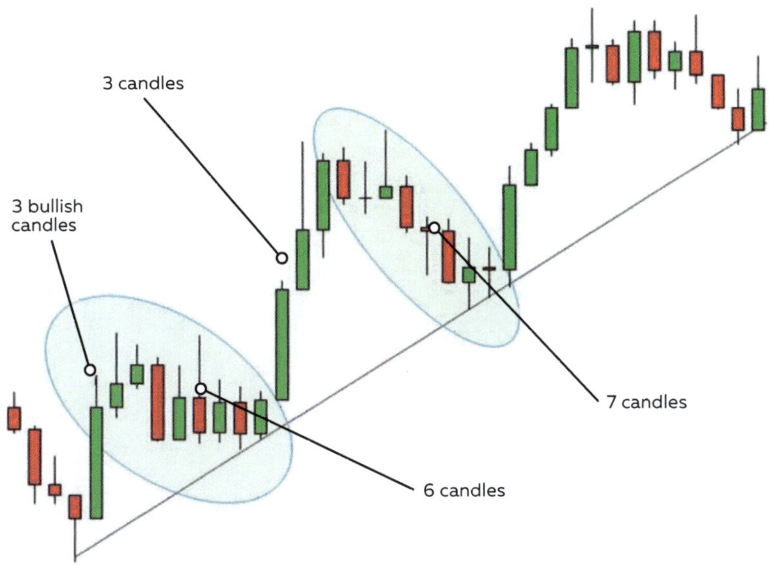

After the price is confirmed, we are more likely to see further upside movement. There are other components that we need to check in our confluences' checklist.

When bulls are in control, normally bears are struggling because the market sentiment doesn't support their territory, and same goes for bearish sentiment. As we look at the picture, you can see that it took a few bullish candles to go up but the accumulation or retracement was slow and it consumed more time than bullish movement usually does.

A 123 structure was presented on the second accumulation, hopefully now you get the picture that we need more components that meet certain criteria to involve ourselves in the market. Note that these examples go hand in hand with other confluences. So, when you look at the market, you can't just use this method alone, other criteria must align. The price that moves during the accumulation or retracement phases are slow. This is common but doesn't happen every time.

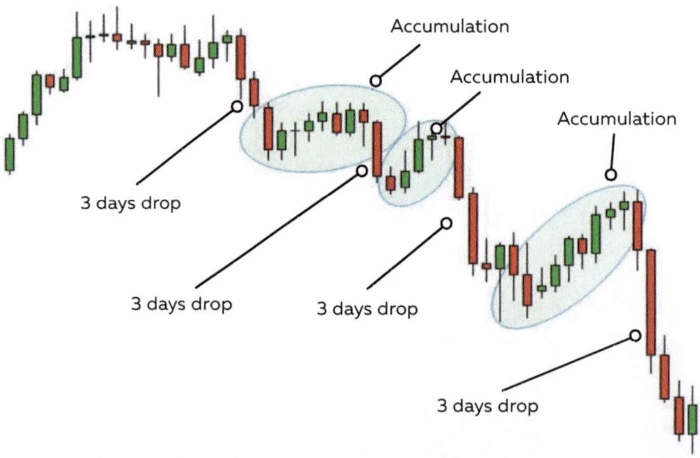

Price broke a support area and turned it into a resistance, which means we need to look for the price to reverse as soon as it gets there. What I like about this setup is it gives us more ideas especially about things we've already mentioned so far.

- Support that was broken and turned into resistance
- 123 structure
- A divergent at the reversal zone

For every accumulation watch out for 123 structures which are more likely to present themselves in those conditions.

6.

1-5
STRUCTURE

This chapter will help you to approach the charts in a mechanical way so you are constantly in tune with right context at play.

6.1 The 1-5 Method

How to identify a 1-5 structure

The market will create a low (1), then last high (2), then break the low (1) and create high (3). As soon as the market breaks higher (2) and creates higher (4), expect a low (5), before further upside movement.

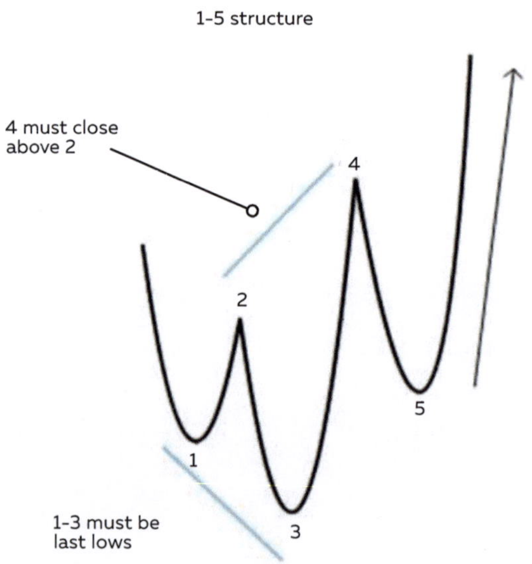

This pattern confluences more or can be used effectively when it appears at the reversal zone.

Note: 1-3 must be last 2 lows, and 4 must close above or below 2.

6.2 Nature of 1-5 structure

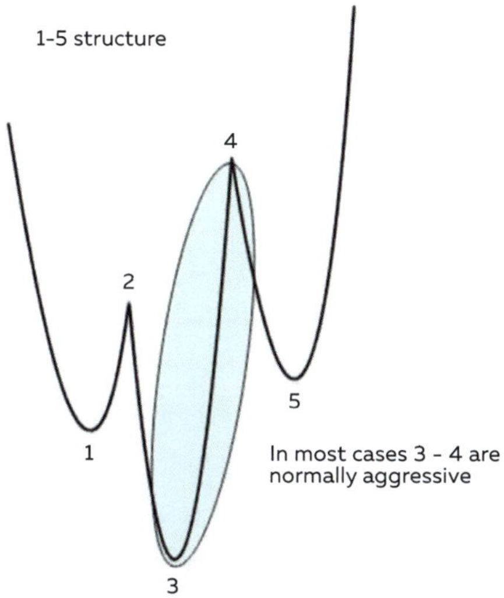

· 3 to 4 moves are aggressive in nature because the price signals the presence of buyers/sellers in the market.

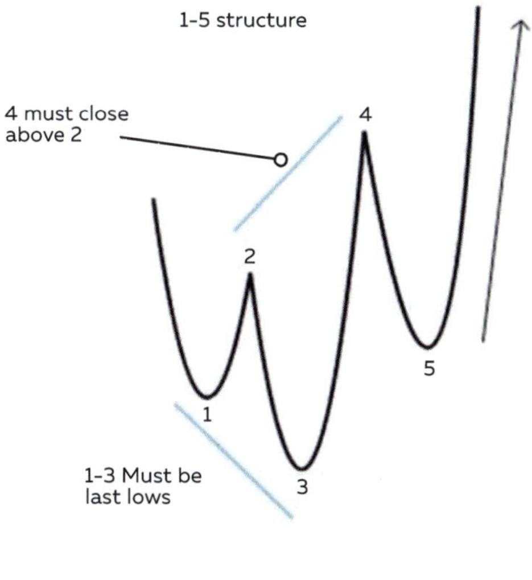

· 4 must close above 2 to show a change of structure.

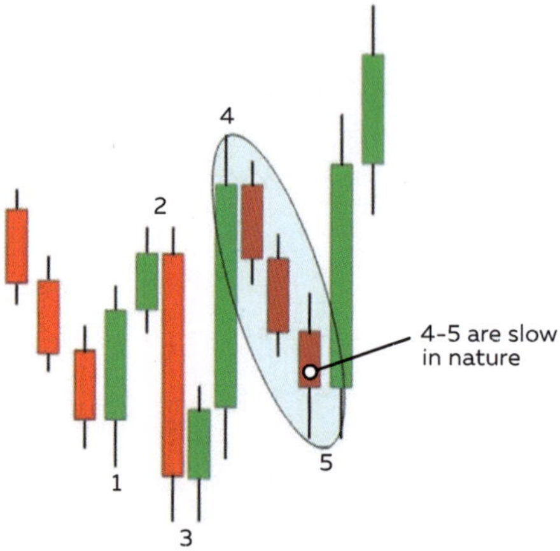

4 to 5 moves are slow in nature and signifies taking profit behavior. After the price reverses, create the 1-5 structure. Once the price reverses from any reversal zone, the 1-5 structure is more likely to present itself and show a change of structure.

6.3 Double 1-5 and triple 1-5 structure

Double 1-5: This happens when you find 2 patterns in different timeframes. You can get a 1-5 on the daily timeframe and 1-5 on a smaller timeframe, but 1-5 from a smaller timeframe will appear at level 5 on a daily timeframe.

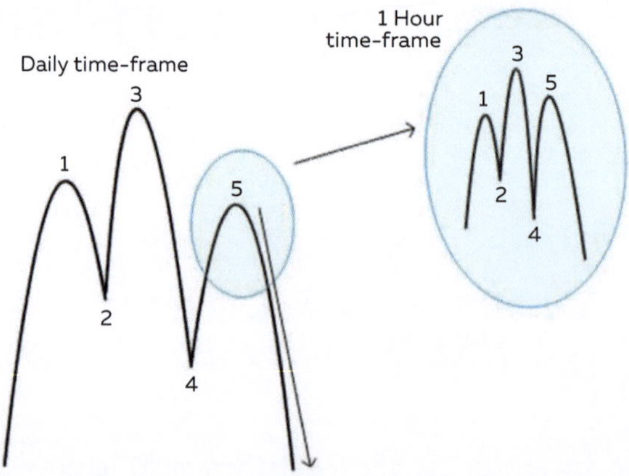

Triple 1-5 structure

We don't normally use this until this point, but a triple 1-5 structure is still useful and can be found in any timeframe. For example: A daily 1-5 followed by a 1-5 on a 1 hour timeframe, will be located at level 5 of a daily timeframe. And 1-5 from 5 or 15 minutes can be found at level 5 of a 1 hour timeframe.

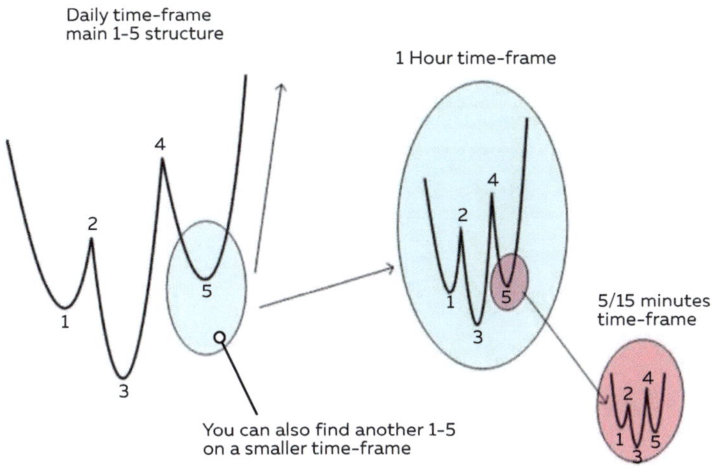

How to trade 1-5 Structure

·Find a reversal zone (Refer to Chapter 1)

·Change of structure (When price break 2 to create 4 and slowly retrace to create 5). Let us take a look at the picture below:

There are 2 reversal zones in the above picture (we consider any 1-5 re-action).

Note: that having many reversal zones must not confuse you, the only thing you need is to watch for reaction at any of your zones. 1-3 create divergent while we wait for price to break 2 and create 4. Since 1-5 happened on a 15 minute timeframe and once price tries to create 5 you can switch to a lower timeframe to look for another 1-5 structure. Note that 5 mostly retrace around 38.2 and 88.0% of Fibonacci retracement, which I will explain in the next chapters.

Above we have a double 1-5, if you look closely. After the price created a 1-4 and while we were waiting for 5 to complete for a buy setup, another 1-5 in that 5 was playing out. Already, this is one of the safest trades to consider.

FIG: 9

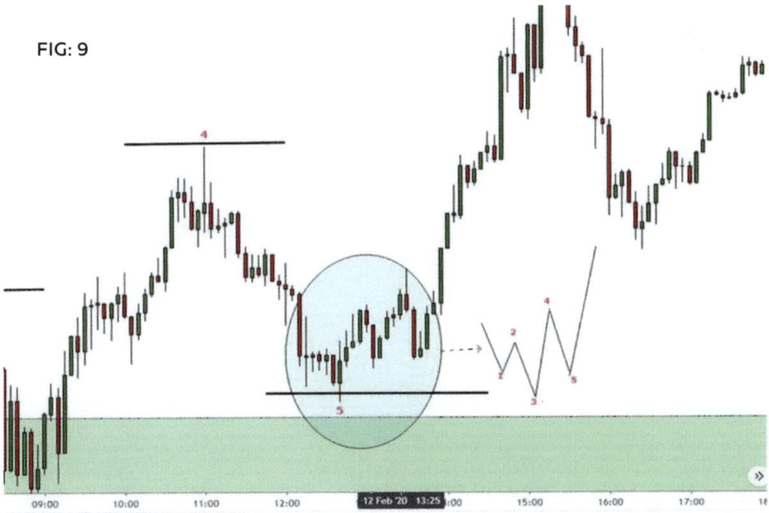

A 1-5 structure and 5 as an entry and below 3 as our stop loss. (Regular 1-5). Note that the reversal zone was found on a 4-hour timeframe and 1-5 structure on a 15 minute timeframe.

How to spot a different 1-5 in different timeframes

(1-5 top down analyses from different timeframes). Look at the diagram: Fig 9 on the previous page, we have a 1-5 on a daily timeframe, and remember that 5 is always our strike zone.

Price broke 2 and creates 4 and retraces back to the support area where we expected a 1-5 reaction to execute our trade.

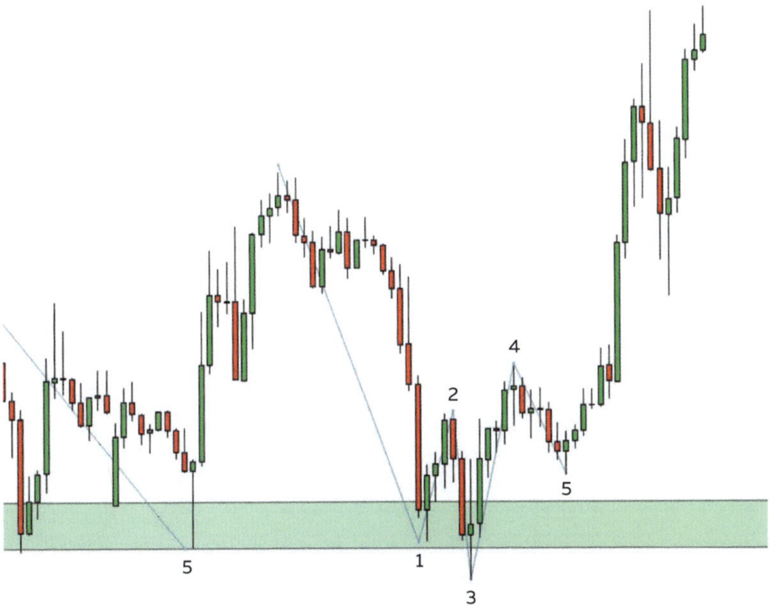

Now that we have our level 5 as our strike or reversal zone, we need to switch to another timeframe where we can find another 1-5 reaction to execute a trade.

6.5 1-5 Structure with Divergent and 123 Structure

4-hour timeframe

We must see 2 and 3 as divergent, remember 3 will act as our last leg of a divergent. This is where we are going to look for a 1-5 structure in another timeframe.

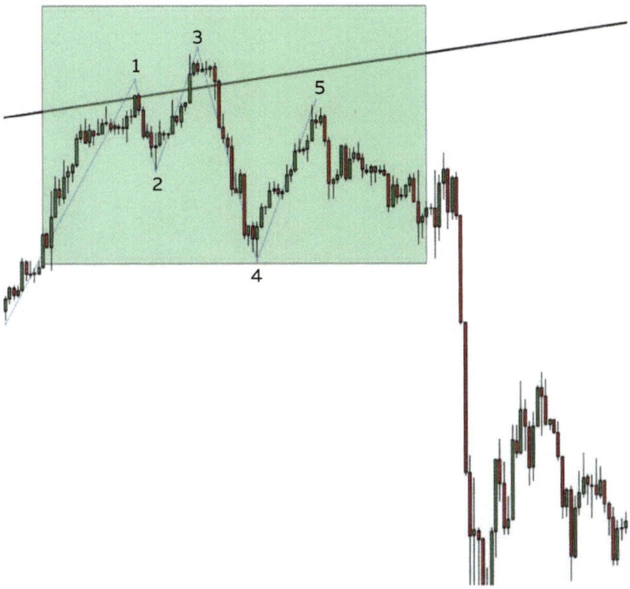

On level 3 we had a beautiful 1-5 structure and 5 as an entry.

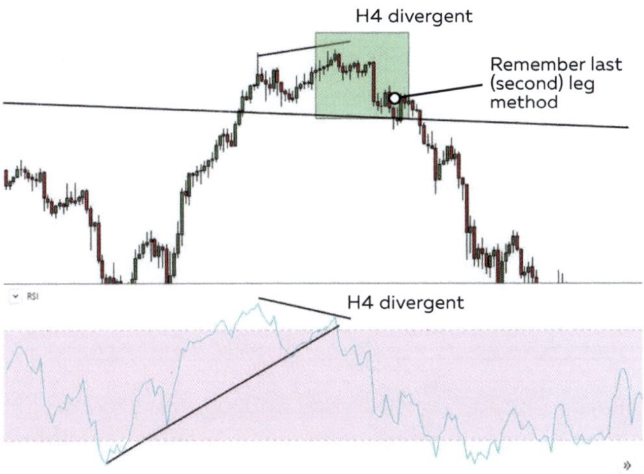

A divergent.

"IT'S NOT WHETHER YOU GET KNOCKED DOWN, IT'S WHETHER YOU GET UP."

Vince Lombardi

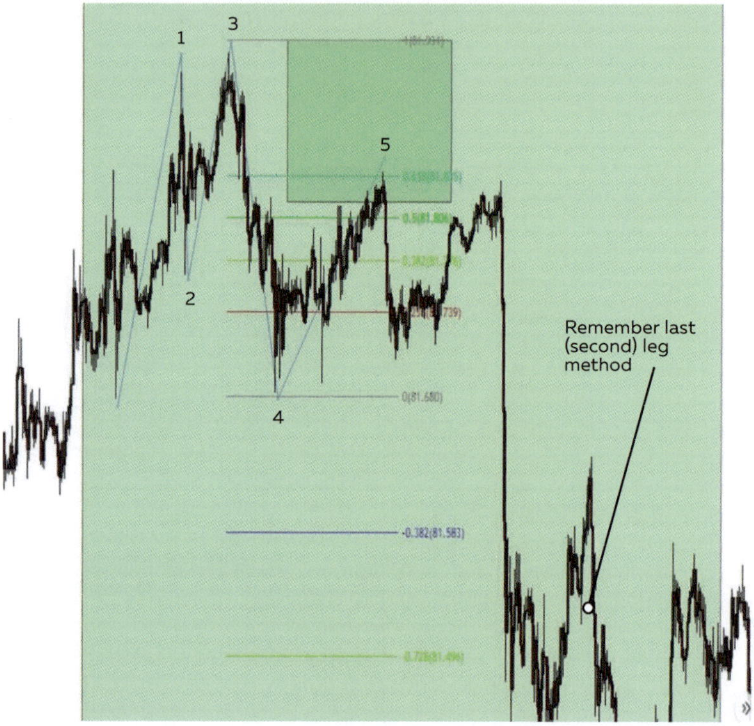

Note that 1 and 3 are almost at the same level, but 3 is an inch above.

6.6 1-5 structure

(Market cycle, 123 structure and trend line)

In this structure, we believe it is important to complete a chapter on market cycle before continuing.

First and foremost, you need to check your monthly timeframe for current market sentiment.

Before price touches a trendline for the third time, we already have an ABCD pattern playing out and D as our potential target. Third touch or third strike is considered as our main zone for buy (reversal zone).

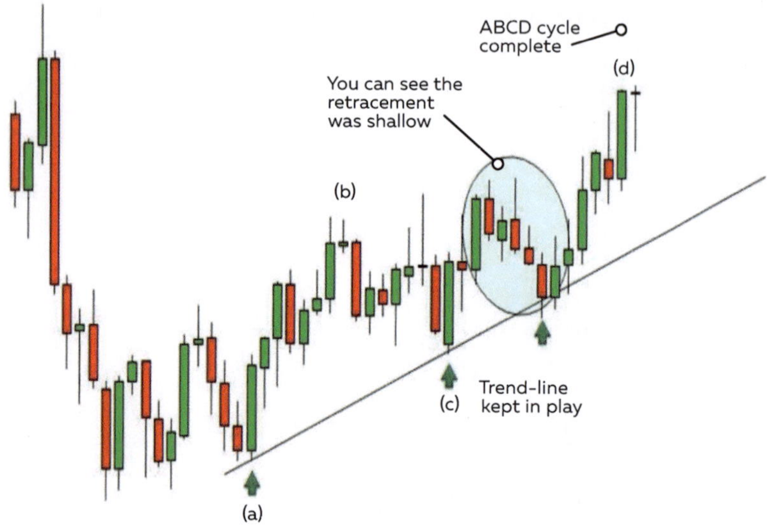
ABCD cycle
complete
(d)
You can see the
retracement
was shallow
(b)
Trend-line
kept in play
(c)
(a)

FIG: 18

You can see the
retracement
was shallow
Trend-line
kept in play

Let us look at the retracement in the diagram: Fig 18 (previous page), since it shows how it retraces towards 3rd strike of a trendline. We have a market cycle in play with this trendline, and we are going to use a 123 structure to see our potential reversal.

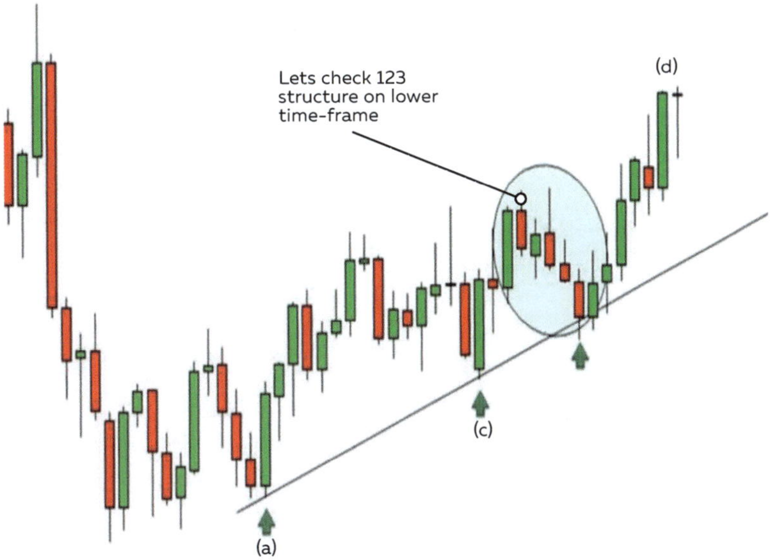

Everything now starts to make sense. There is a 123 structure inside that we ignore because there was no divergent at all. 2 And 3 is where the divergent took place and 1-3 will be our last price before price level 2 to create 4 and 5 to be our entry zone. We can take trades around 3 of a 123 structure with a divergent in play and other trades around 5 of 1-5 structure.

A SIMPLE SUPPLY ZONE AND 1-5 STRUCTURE

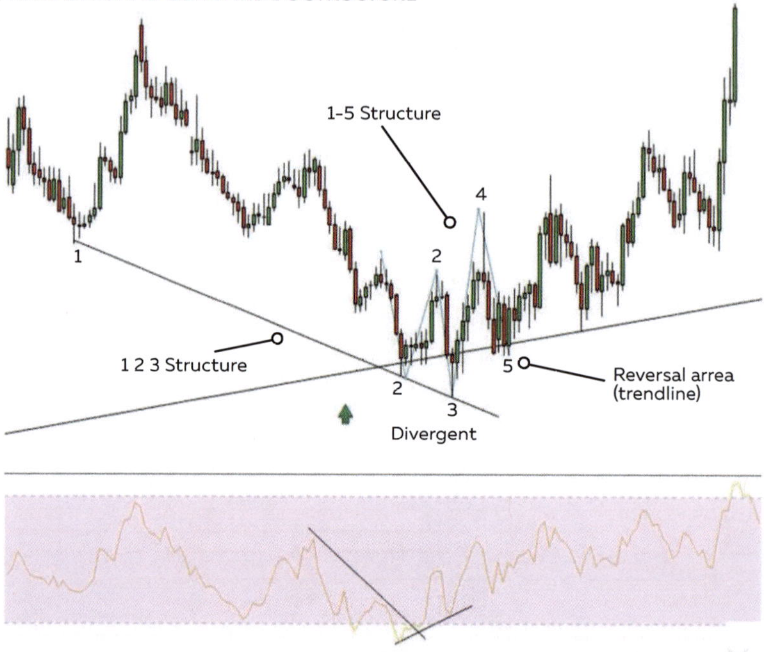

Another simple supply zone and 1-5 structure. We already know the rules of a trendline break that creates a zone. In this case the supply zone was created and the last bullish candle was covered before price drop and revisited again for a sell setup.

6.7 Entry, Stop Loss and Take Profit

Sell setup

After price touches a reversal zone, we wait for a 1-5 structure to present itself, a 5 for our entry and 3 as our stop loss. Your stop loss must be not at level 3 exactly, is should be at least 30 pips away depending on the currency you will be trading. Risk management must be considered.

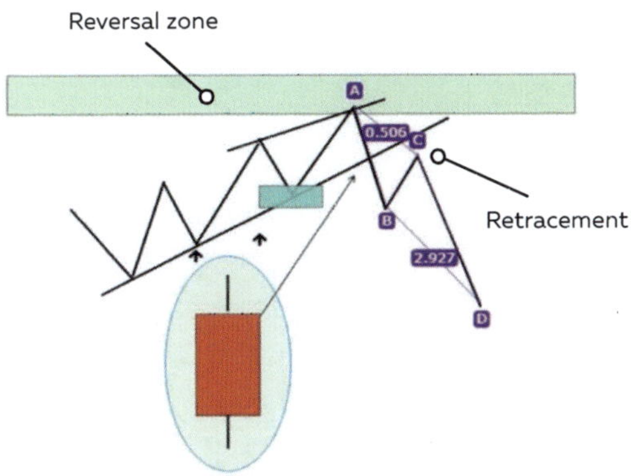

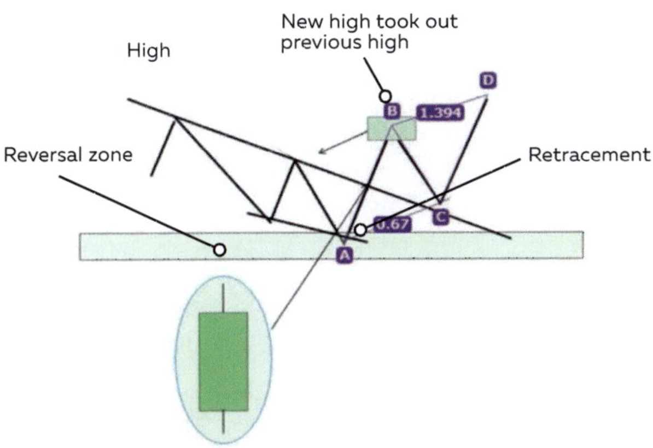

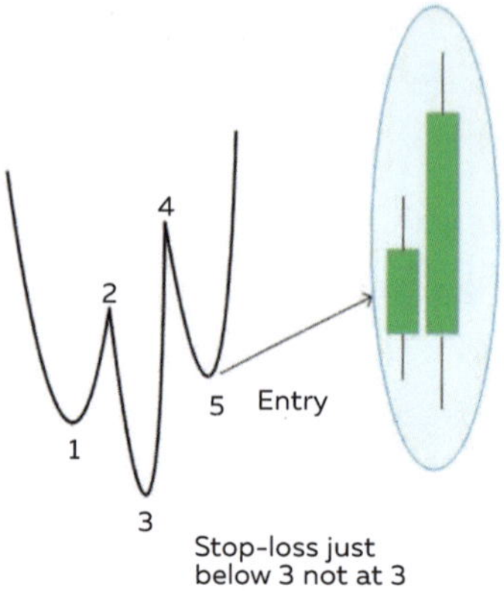

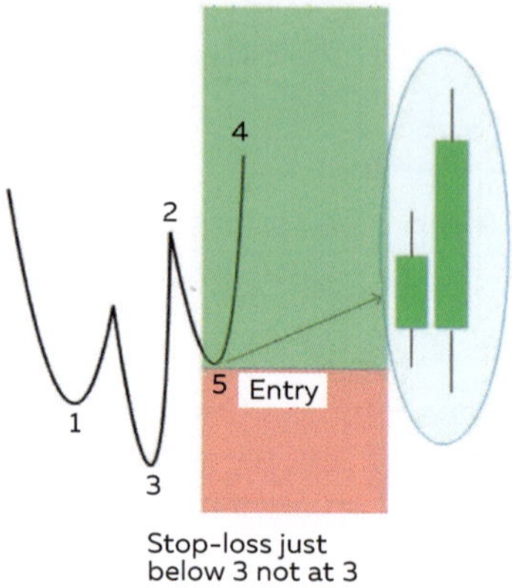

Trendline and 1-5 Structure

There's always a wait in everything. You can try to avoid such setups by waiting to see a proper reaction before you do anything.

If price breaks a trendline without a proper reaction, it is better to wait for the price to give you what you looking for.

The below pictures show a preferable structure to trade a trendline. We already know how to draw a trendline and third touch as our entry zone. To avoid taking bad trades, its advisable to trade third touch after we see a sign of a 1-5 structure.

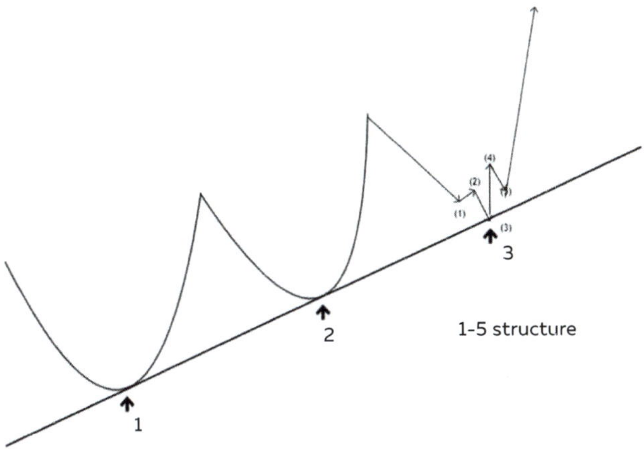

We have highs being created, a trendline in play, a break of resistance, a clean break to consider and a retest to a new support area. A retest that confluences with a third touch and 1-5 structure.

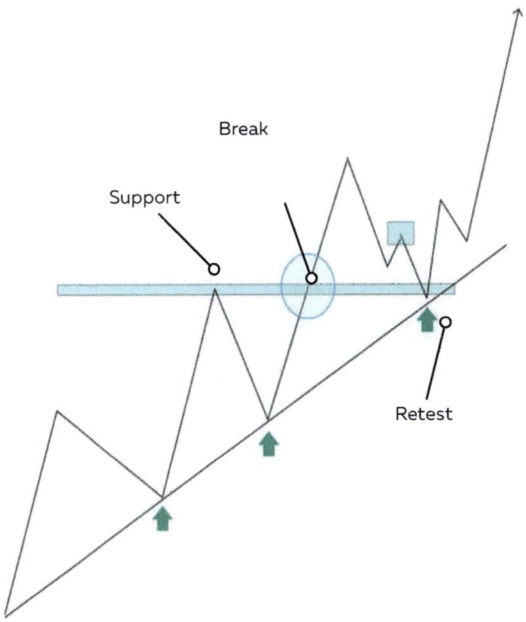

7.

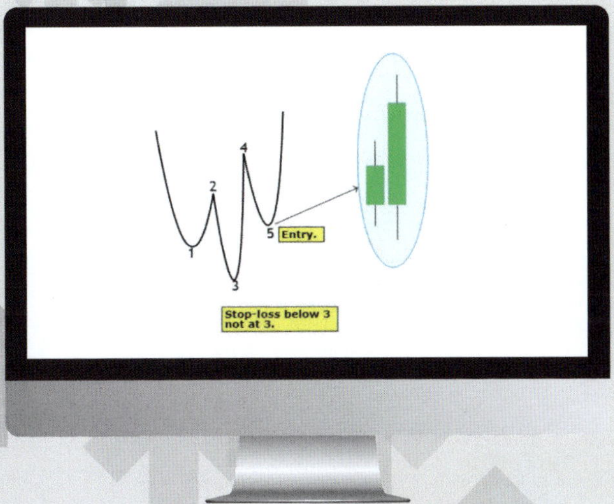

FIBONACCI TRADING

Apart from the historical importance, we will now look at the Fibonacci sequence of numbers and the associated 'Golden Ratio' manifesting in nature and in certain works of art (Logarithmic spiral series). We have to understand that everything in the universe is governed by law and order, meaning that even in the financial market nothing moves by mistake. For every cause there will be an effect. Fibonacci numbers are infinite but we will only be working with a few important numbers.

We have fib retracement that indicate the possible levels the price can retrace, resume to its direction and fib extension which will serve as a price projection for possible target.

Fibonacci Retracement

(0.236 = 23.6) Will be explained separately.

(0.382 = 38.2)

(50.0 = 50.0)

(61.8 = 61.8)

Fibonacci Extension

-38.20 = 138.2

-61.80 = 161.8

Before we can start using these numbers, we need to revisit some basics for those who are new to this tool. We all know that when a price creates highs/lows there are chances that we might see more highs/lows. How do we time that? That is where the Fibonacci sequence comes in.

Bullish Retracement

Once we have identified the market sentiment, we can start to look for retracements. After price created a new high, we normally look for retracement before another new high. The Fibonacci will be drawn from a previous low to latest new high, remember in this case we will be looking for a retracement so we can buy hoping for a continuation of the market.

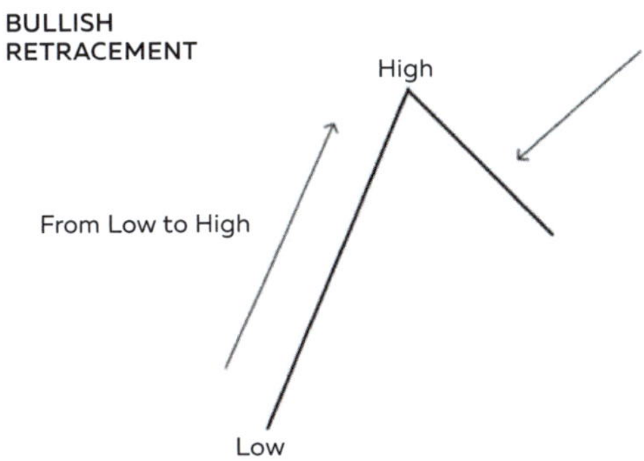

Price creating a new high

We must wait for a new high to complete before we can consider it as a new high, there is a new bearish candle retracing opposite, we

need to see at least 30% of price going against the initial bullish move, starting from the previous low.

We can start plotting our Fibonacci once the price goes through the 23.6% and 38.2% zone which qualifies it as a retracement. Once the price dips through the two zones, then we immediately start looking at what price can do around 50.0% and 61.8% Fibonacci retracement level.

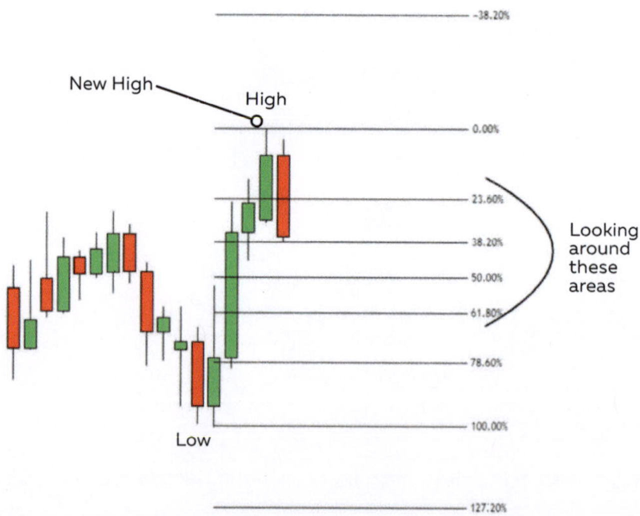

In most cases price retrace around (38.2, 50.0 and 61.8) which are regarded as our reversal zones, we have learned so far that when price reaches reversal zone, we do not just execute our trade we need confirmations that will be explained as we go, in this case we just doing an example. It is usually around the 38.20, 50.0 and 61.8% levels that we are more likely going to see the market retracing and buyers coming in to push the price further up.

Eventually price went up to create another new high.

As price keeps moving higher, we are expecting the same behavior that happened previously, for every new high, we are more likely to see a retracement again.

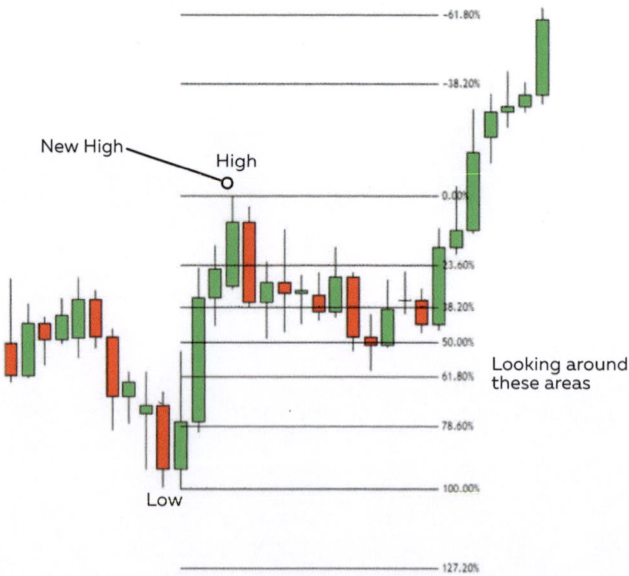

Another new high has been created.

We draw our Fibonacci from our latest low to our new high looking at the areas of reversals zone. (38.0, 50.0 and 61.8%) to buy again.

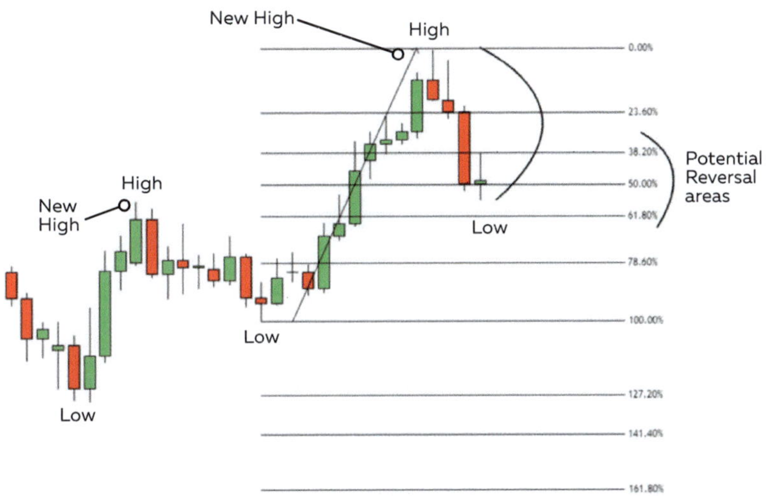

Price continued going up again, we will repeat this procedure until price reaches our major reversal zone or market changes its market sentiment, the idea is to identify the trend and trade along with, Fibonacci is a tool to help us with all that.

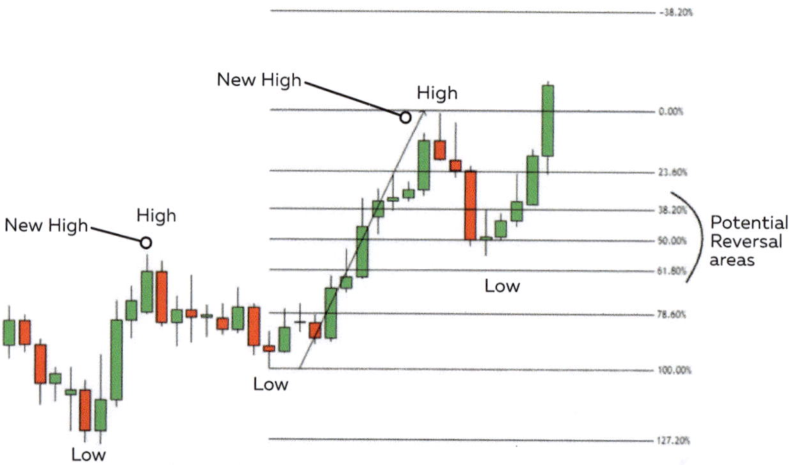

Bearish Retracement

There is not much difference between how we use our Fibonacci for a bull or a bearish market except changing the way we plot it, from a bearish perspective we draw it from the previous high to our recent low.

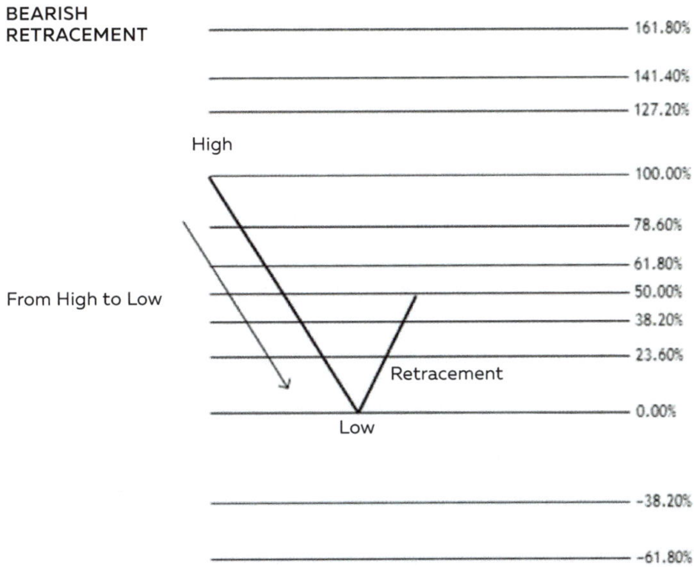

Price dropped and created a new low, we expect a bit of a retracement before we start plotting our Fibonacci.

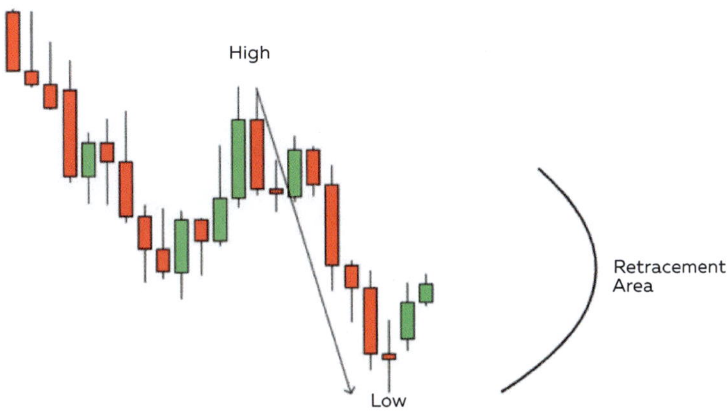

Draw your Fibonacci from previous high to get a retracement area.

There is another aspect that needs to be taken into consideration, because we tend to get support/resistance and supply and demand next to each other, we always advice that we consider the last zone, unless you are having more proper confluence around the first reversal zone. After we drew our Fibonacci, we see price approaching resistance, but the trick is: we have a supply zone above. With experience you will encounter these trends in the market.

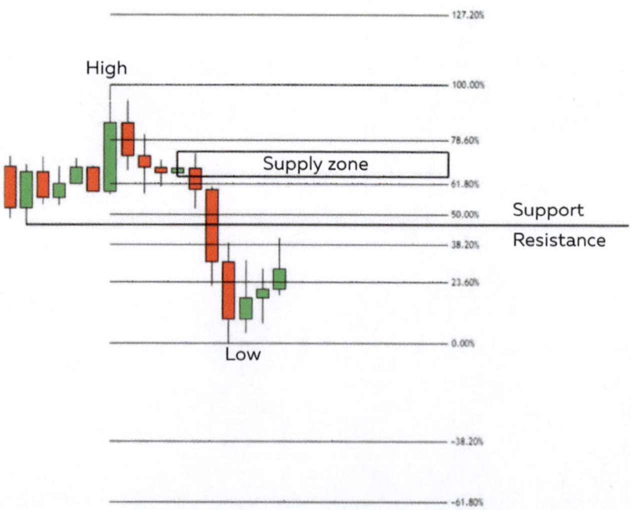

The price ignored resistance and went in our supply zone before we saw price reaching from that zone before dropping. Sometimes price can reverse around any area that confluences with resistance, therefore have a clear reason why you are entering the trade.

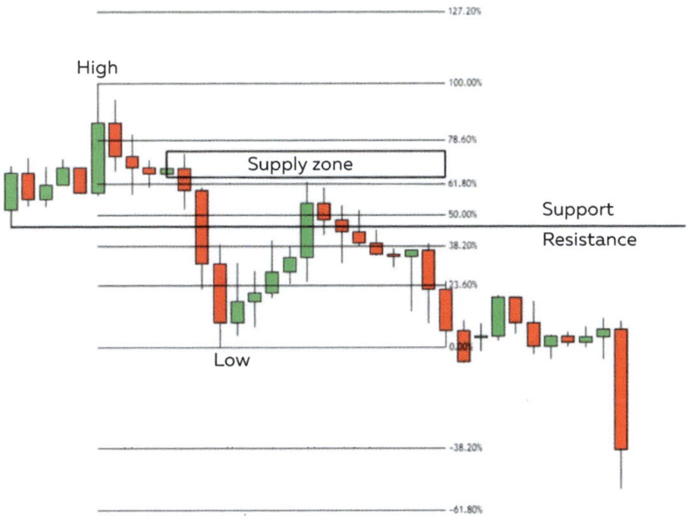

Price bounce at our area of reversal, the question will be about our ideal target and more entries going up or down. In this case let us say we on the bigger timeframe, obviously after price retraced around 61.8%, price might take longer to reach our target, normally from 61.8 % going up, there will be a series of highs and lows developing toward the extension target.

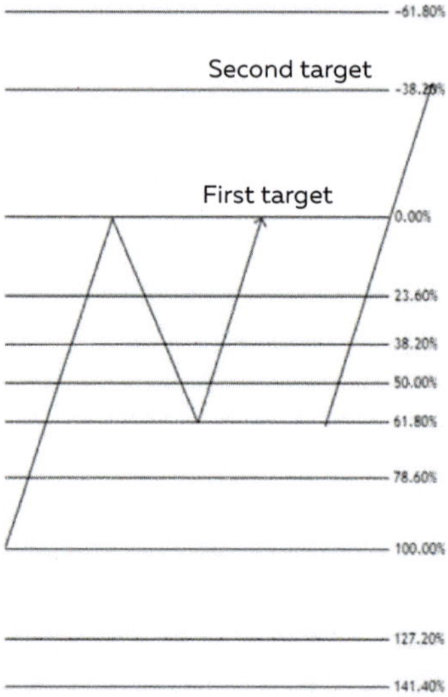

-61.80%
Second target
-38.20%
First target
0.00%
23.60%
38.20%
50.00%
61.80%
78.60%
100.00%
127.20%
141.40%

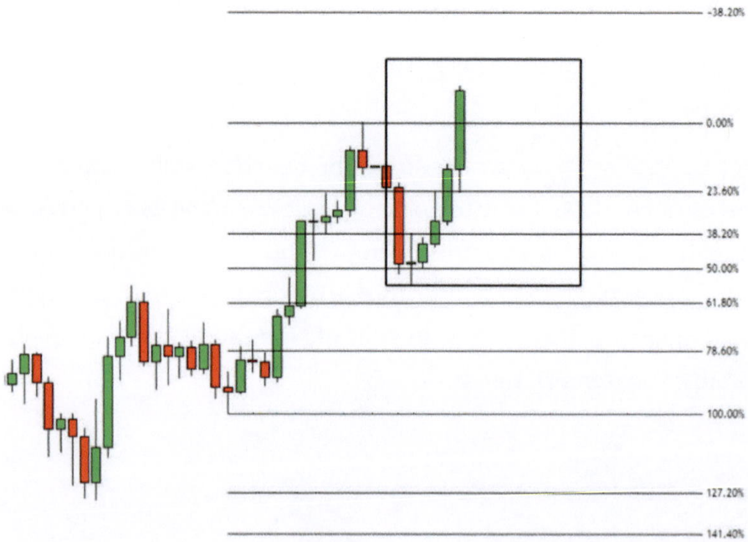

-38.20%
0.00%
23.60%
38.20%
50.00%
61.80%
78.60%
100.00%
127.20%
141.40%

Bigger timeframe

When price respects our reversal zone and confirms a continuation, there will be other retracements that will develop along the way.

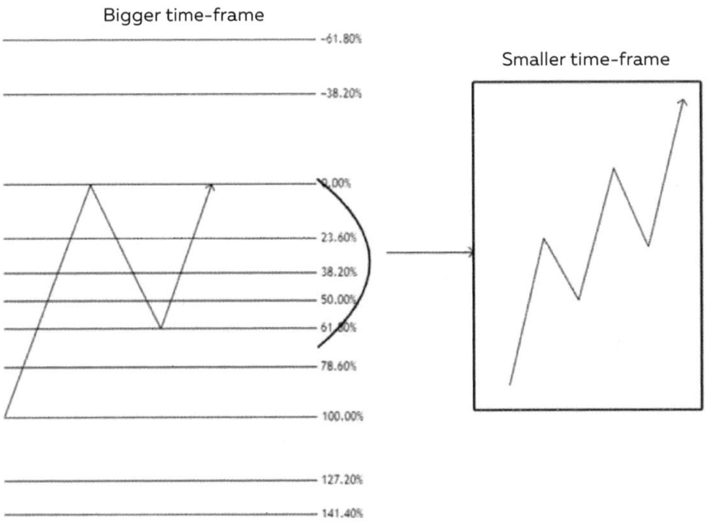

Lower timeframe and its more highs and lows.

"FAILURE WILL NEVER OVERTAKE ME IF MY DETERMINATION TO SUCCEED IS STRONG ENOUGH."

Og Mandino

Now we know how to draw a Fibonacci. At this moment we are going to focus on 38, 50 and 61.8 Fibonacci retracement.

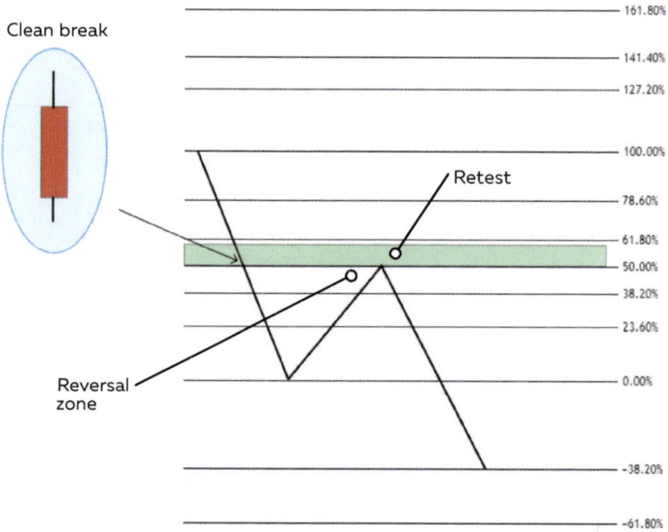

Before price reached any Fibonacci level that we mentioned, we must take other confluences into consideration, we now know that with every low or high there will be a possible next low or high and for every break probably a retest will follow.

Here are some examples before we dive into other necessary confluences. This is a basic structure where we will consider a couple of things, the support was broken and a clean break determines a strong sentiment to that break and the retest follows.

DOUBLE BOTTOM

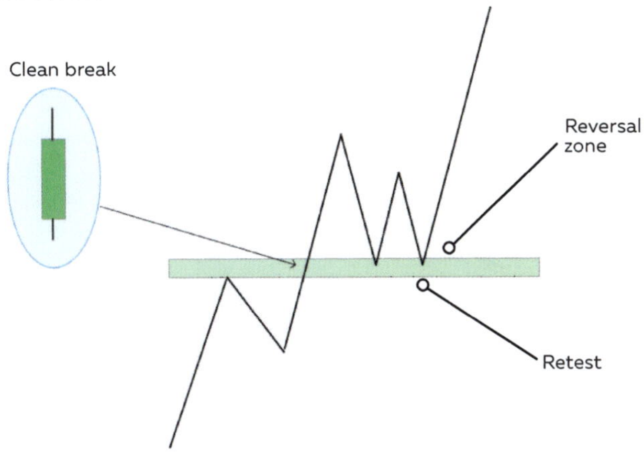

TRIPLE BOTTOM

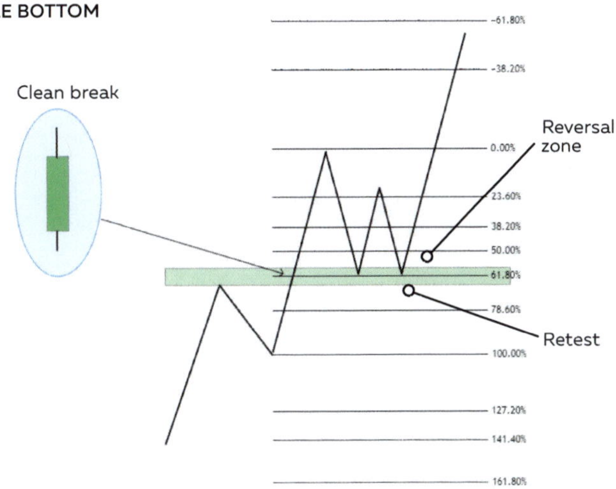

Fibonacci levels act as key areas (support and resistance) in most cases, the bigger the timeframe the better. Fibonacci levels can hold the price before resuming with a trend.

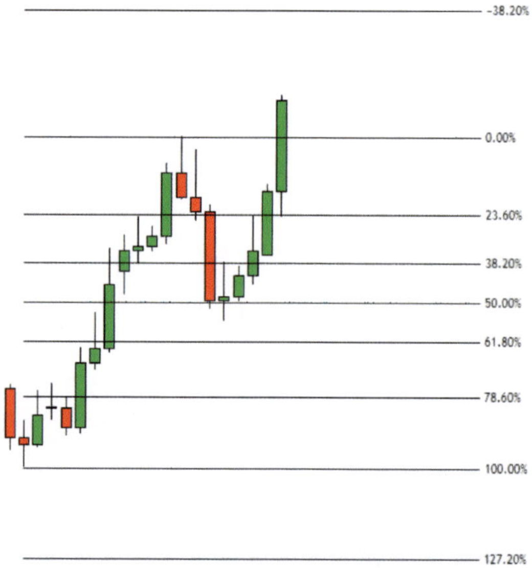

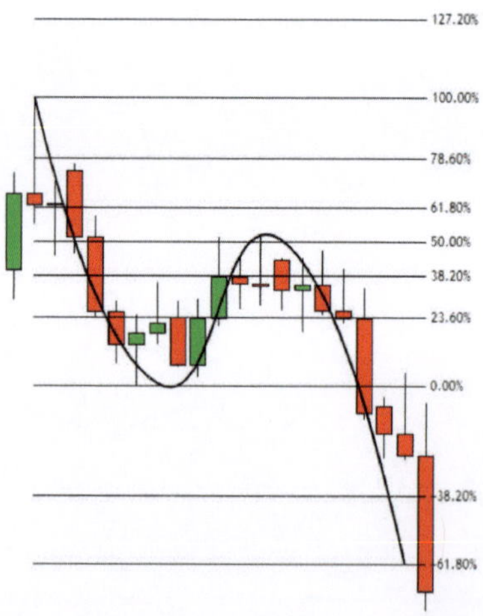

Let's go into detail, as we go, the price went up before Fibonacci was drawn or used, it hit 50.0% level twice before it resumed with a trend, and you can buy around the area where price held, in this scenario we are working with 50.0% as an entry, and below 61.8% fib level as our stop loss and -38.20% as our first target.

I can't explain Fibonacci extension separately, because it's an easy concept to grasp, so we will mix it with retracement. Fibonacci extension serve as a price projection for possible target and reversal only if it confluences with any major reversal zones.

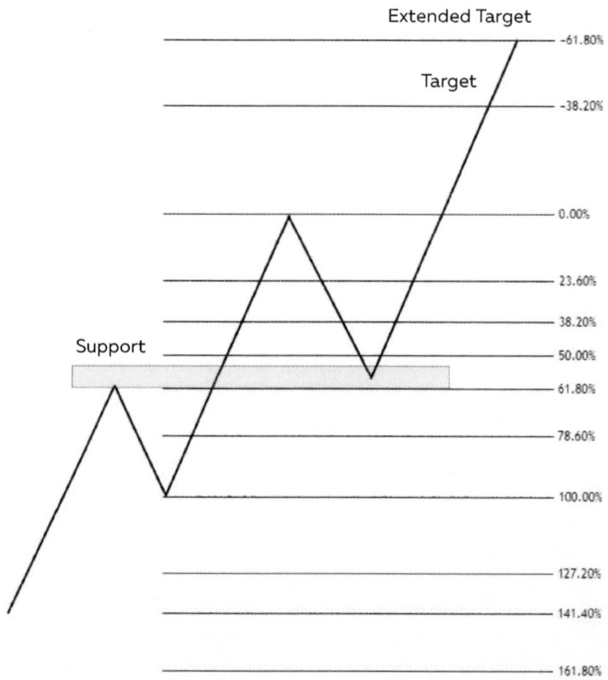

The above diagram shows a basic market making highs until the target 38.20 and -61.80.

The picture contains almost every confluence we need before taking any trade. Price broke previous high with what we call a clean break (remember a clean break must be convincing that there are more buyers in the house), price created a new high and a shallow retracement towards our reversal zone, we had price stuck around 23.60%whichwasignored,thenwestarttopayattentionfrom38.20% where it confluences with a previous resistance which is new support. Price broke our counter trendline, with candlestick confirmation.

After the price left reversal zone, we now focus on our possible target which is -38.20% and -61.8.

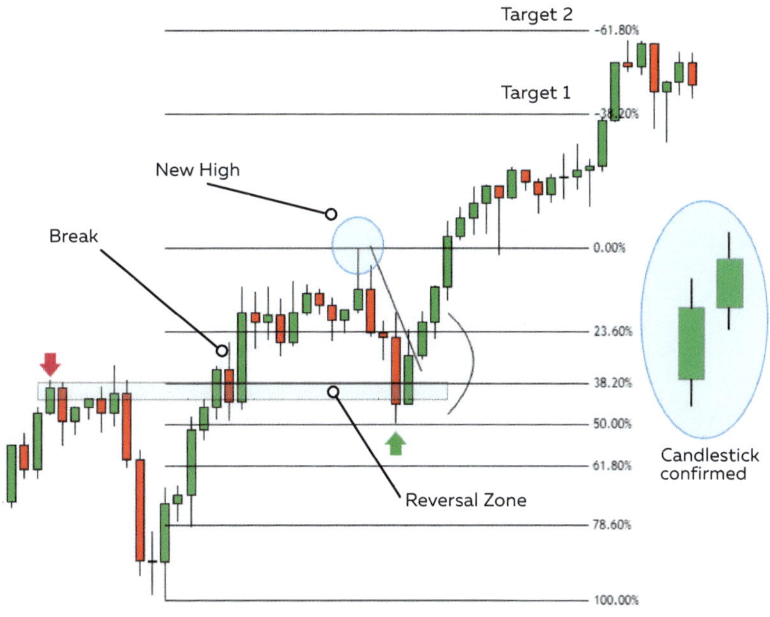

Price rejected around 50.0% and went straight to -61.80% and reversed (note that we only take reversal at -38.20 and 61.8% if there is a reversal zone only).

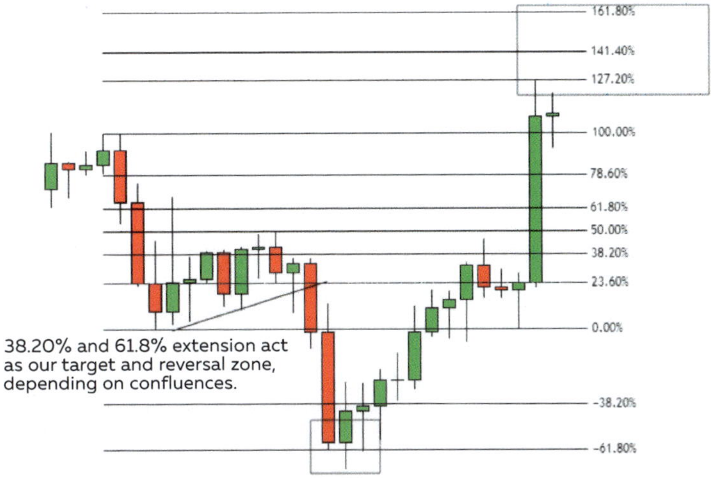

Price dropped and retraced back to 61.8 Fibonacci retracement, tested twice and breaks a counter trendline and falls.

We are not going to explain too much about failed setups, because we all know that in this business we speculate and anticipate, nothing is certain.

In the below picture price gave us what we normally look for, it dropped but never reached our potential target. The market will do these kind of things sometimes. It can take you out before continuing in a direction you anticipated, sometimes never reaching entry or target level, and that's part of the game. Entering a trade is one thing and managing it is another. The most important thing is Risk Reward Ratio. Know that the majority of traders don't have enough patience, but by maintaining our risk, the Risk Reward Ratio will keep us in the market for a longer time. It is advisable after every breakeven to try and make at least twice what you have risked. So if you going to risk $100 at least then, you should be willing make $200. This is the correct way to manage risk.

23.60% Fibonacci level. (As a Fake out)

Not so many traders use 23.60% Fibonacci level as far as I've seen. We did mention 38.2, 50 and 61.8%. We going to trade 23.60% as a trap setup, not that it can't be traded but mostly it comes with a lot of false signals (trap acting as a continuation) that we can use them to our advantage.

Basic Trap Setup

Price bounce around 23.60% level and resume above high, the last high where the fib level was placed, you don't have to remove the Fibonacci to (2). After the price broke the high it came back for 61.8%, sometimes it can be 38.20% or 50.0% base on reversal zone.

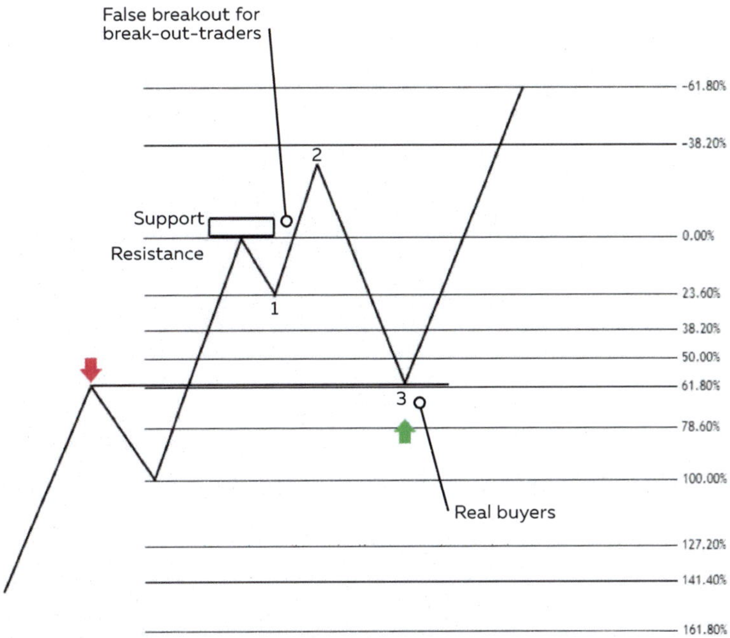

Example 1

In this picture price retraced around 50.0% because of a reversal zone. (Demand zone)

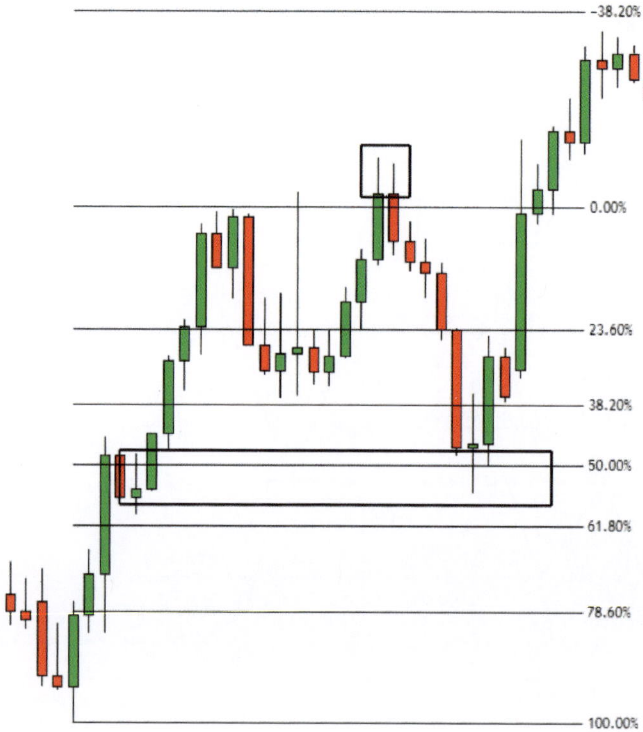

Example 2

This is a 1-5 structure of 23.60% Fibonacci level. 1-2 (Plotting of Fibonacci hoping for a retracement) price retraces to 23.60% and continues to break the high where buyers think it's a breakout and a continuation from the 1-2 initial move. The price starts to retrace back, and breaks (3). Thereafter, buyers stops are taken before price retraced to our mostly used areas of retracement before taking off.

Example 3

Price went up and retraced around 23.60% before aggressively breaking the high and retest, convincing more buyers to buy hoping for a continuation then price start to slowly retrace back in and take buyers stop-loss' before real buyers come in the market.

In this case we see our normal 123 structure playing out at our reversal zone (Fibonacci levels).

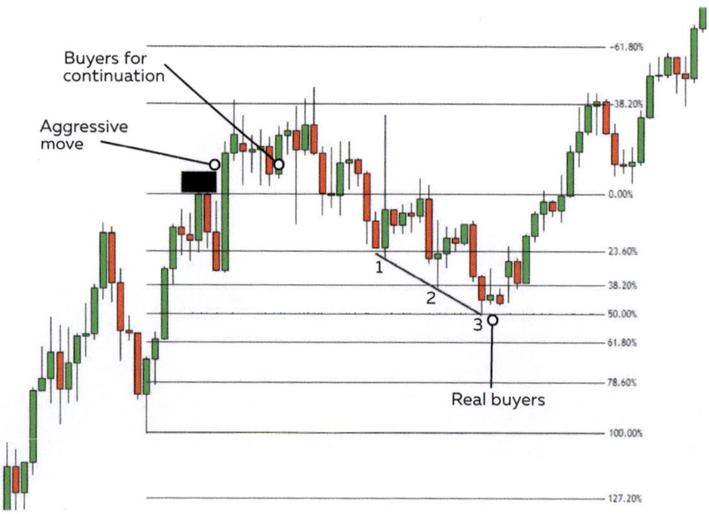

Example 4

Another false sell setup at 23.60%. Price created some sort of a resistance, acting as a continuation that led many sellers to come in the market before a huge one bullish candle corrects the situation and weak sellers (small stop loss) where taken out. Price held 50.0% Fibonacci level nicely before real sellers take over.

8.

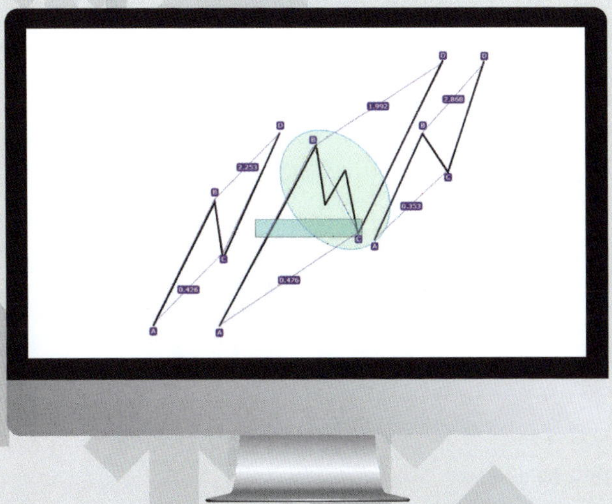

MARKET CYCLES

ABCD structure as cycle

An ABCD structure has been out there for a while and has many explanations. In this chapter we will try to explain different structures with cycles. A major cycle is found on a monthly timeframe. Before you think of taking a trade, a monthly timeframe must be conspired before anything else.

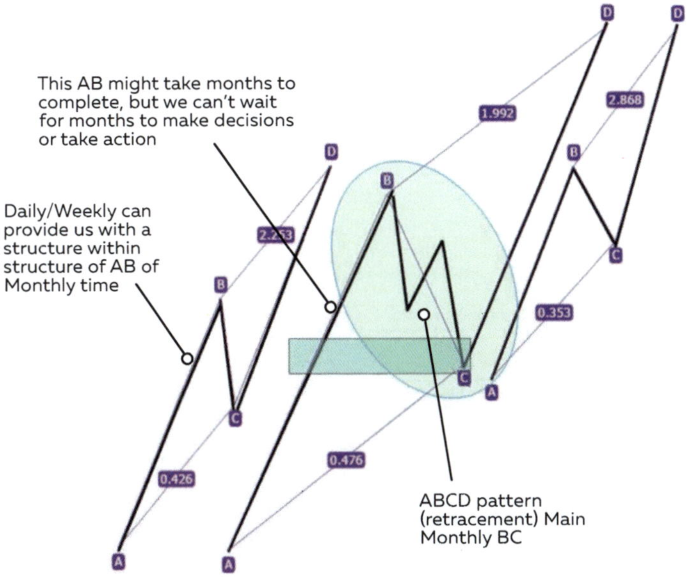

AB is leading (motive) smoothly in the direction of a trend (Big but less candles).

BC retracement is compulsive in nature, sloppy and slow (Small and more candles).

CD resuming of AB motive move, target: measure AB distance is equal to CD. Fib level: 38.2, 50.0, 61.8

Let us take a look at an AB move. It can be just a move in a monthly timeframe, but on weekly and daily timeframes it's another story.

Weekly timeframe – you can automatically see a series of ABCD structure, since the market is creating highs and low.

A labeled weekly timeframe

Don't get confused by the way I have labeled this. Remember a cycle within a cycle, when another cycle ends, there is already one in play.

What to look at when trading ABCD structure

There are many confluences that we did cover in another chapter.

- After price created (A) ,a trendline was set. It breaks a support area – it is important to have a clean break that proves the presence of strong seller/buyers in the market.
  B is our retracement, its slower and requires more patience (counter sentiment) on a smaller timeframe you will see it stick to a trendline that has created a drop (A) which confluences with:
- Resistances since price broke support
- C will be viewed as our reversal zone and this is where 123 and 1-5 methods should be considered.

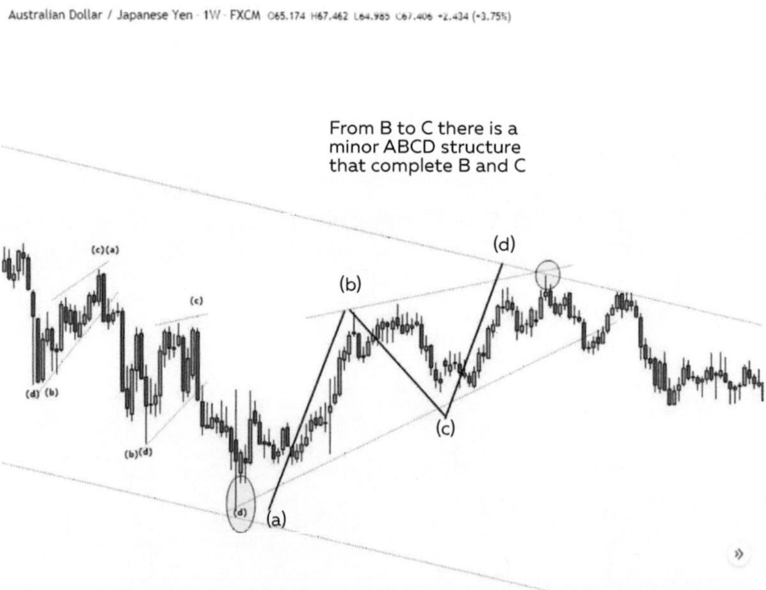

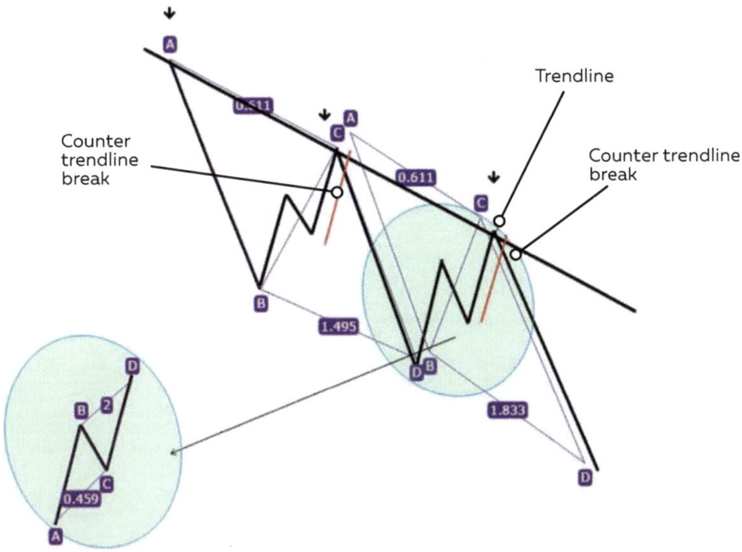

Counter Trendline + Main Trendline + Counter Trendline

We did cover trendline rules and how it can be used. From A to B will be our first impulsive move, followed by B and C as retracement, for entry purpose we going to use a counter trendline and target D for a profit taking zone.

In the following scenario we are expecting a touch on a trendline (3rd strike).

Since it's a monthly/weekly trendline it might take some time to react on our trendline, but in other small timeframes the market is creating highs and lows through the ABCD pattern.

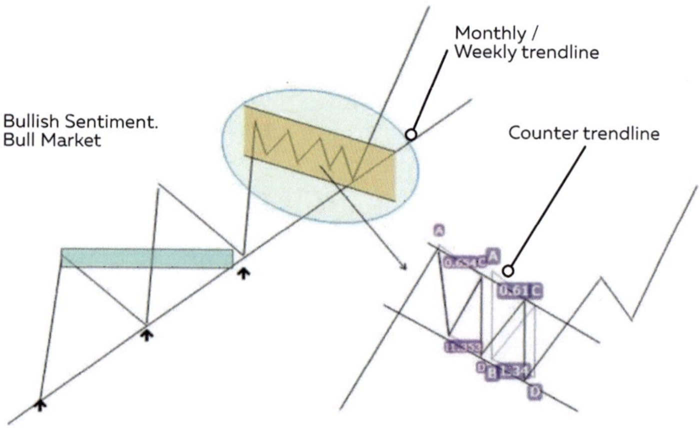

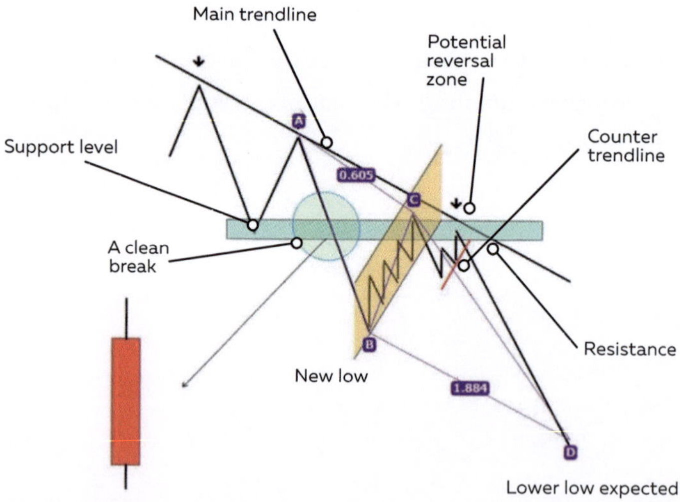

We emphasise a clean break for any level (support and resistance). Checklist – support and resistance + clean break. Retest confluences with (C level, resistance + 3rd strike of trendline).

Counter trendline - hopefully at this point things are making sense.

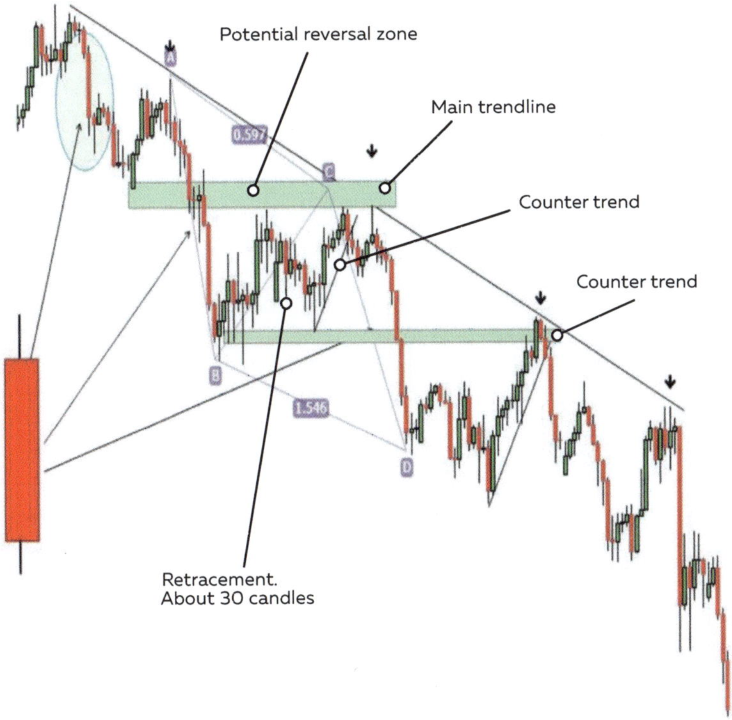

The most important thing is the behavior of the first retracement (more candles) before the price resumes.

"THE MARKET CAN STAY IRRATIONAL LONGER THAN YOU CAN STAY SOLVENT."

John Maynard Keynes

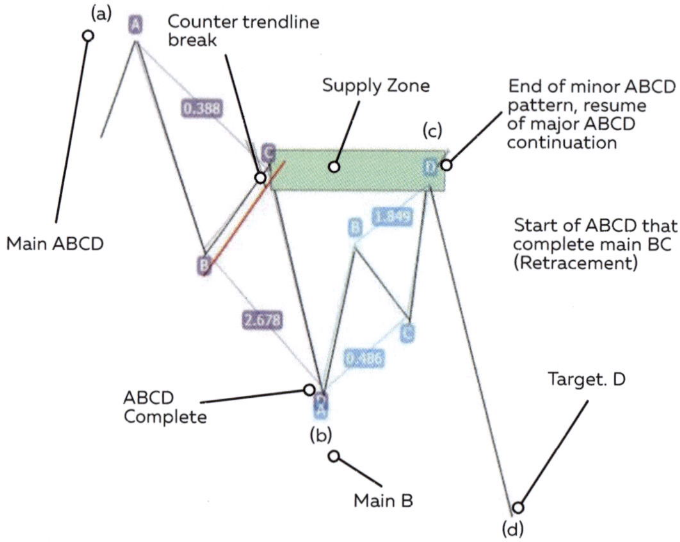

Main ABCD

Within major AB there is ABCD structure in play. (It is not easy to identify AB while is in play). After the price completed AB, it will try to retrace and create C before a major reversal and in that major C there will be minor ABCD structure to C.

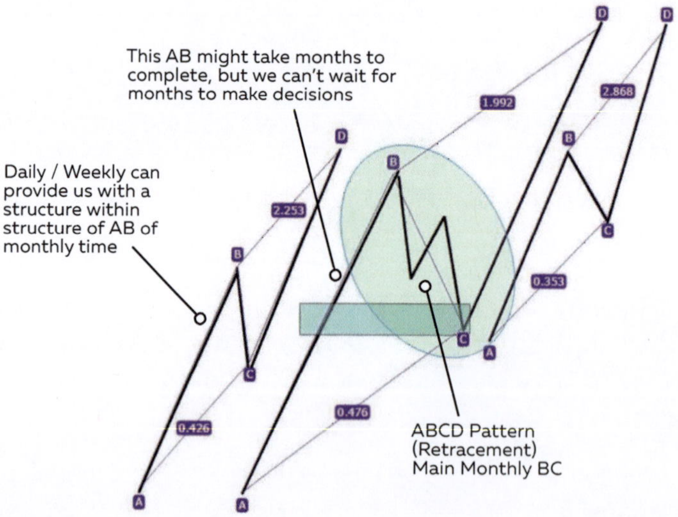

On a high timeframe AB might take months to form and complete, but we can't wait for months to make any decisions.
Daily/weekly timeframes can provide us with a structure within a structure of monthly AB as ABCD. Same goes with C, there will be an ABC and with D too.

How to Gauge the Strength of a Currency and Use it to Your Advantage

Almost every major currency has a currency index, which in a measure changes in the value of the currency. Many traders usually use the Dollar Index to track pairs like USDCHF, USDJPY, EURUSD, GBPUSD etc. When a certain currency index gains strength, you know that currency will gain strength too.

For an example, if the Dollar Index is gaining strength, it means a strong USD, and when it loses strength, the USD weakens. More practical examples will follow.

Index code for other currencies:

CXY = CANADIAN DOLLAR
JXY = JAPANESS YEN
AXY = AUSTRALIAN DOLLAR
DXY = DOLLAR INDEX
SXY = SWISS INDEX
EXY = EUROPEAN INDEX
ZXY = NEW ZEALAND INDEX

The price bounced in the demand zone (Reversal zone). If the price was bearish towards a reversal zone, we can expect some reaction when the price gets into that reversal zone and changes the direction. What will be the outcome in this for NZD? NZD will gain strength.

Trade setup to look for.

Sell XXXNZD Buy NZDXXX

GBP / NZD

The pair's sentiment was bullish until the price broke the uptrend trendline. Since the ZXY (New Zealand Index) indicated that there was opportunity for the NZD to strengthen, this gave us a projection of a bearish sentiment for XXXNZD, and technically we can start to look for sell patterns or sell opportunities.

When you go to a lower timeframe, the price broke a short term trendline, retest and short for almost 30days of bearish.

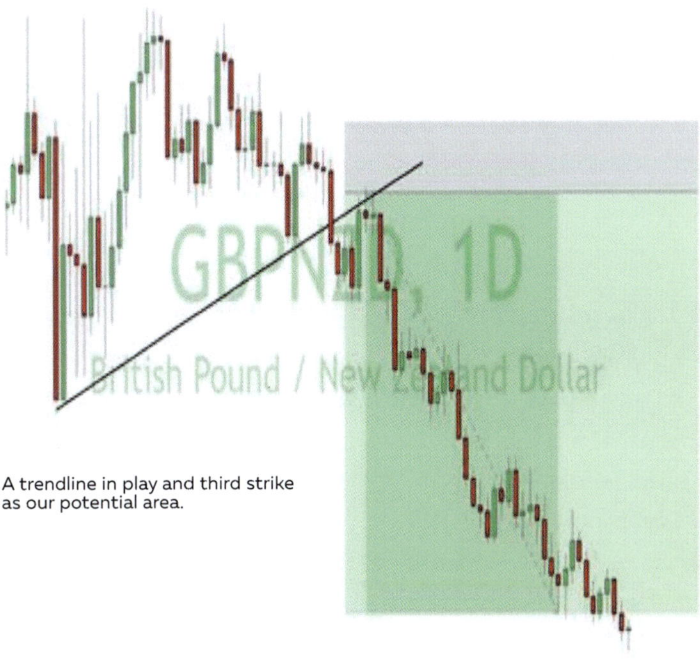

A trendline in play and third strike as our potential area.

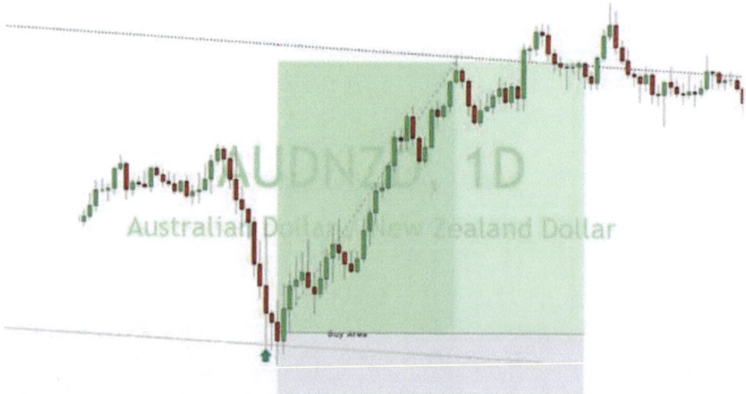

Over the past 15 months the Swiss Index has been bullish, indicating some bullish strength for CHF currency, with highs and lows in play. We did mention that when the market creates a high/low there are chances that another high/low will follow.

Outcome for CHF

Strength for CHF

XXXCHF Sell CHFXXX Buy

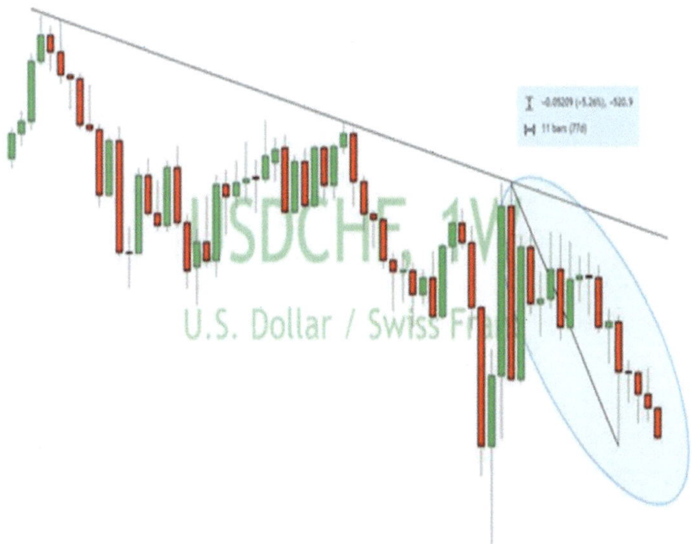

Is this case scenario we have Japanese Yen Index, the instrument had been ranging for over 40 months, which indicated nothing good about the Japanese currency, because as we know currency is the mirror of a country's economy.

When we look at the likes of the JPY against the USD, there wasn't much good trading going on over there.

CXY= Canadian Dollar Index.

How many times would you take a trade if it ranges the whole week or month? In this market you need to be smart, you have to pair the weakest with the strongest. Looking at a currency's economy helps a lot - especially when you look at what their GDP is and what is the major contributor. Some countries rely on mining, manufacturing or agriculture, and a bad or good performance can help a currency gain or lose strength - but that's a topic for another day, it requires a book on its own.

9.

CONFLUENCES & GUIDELINES

CONFLUENCES

Confluences are like a recipe, you need certain ingredients before you can have a specific meal of your choice - same with trading, you'll also need tools and specific reasons for making any trade.

You can't just wake up and take a trade, not if you want to make a winning trade. Being able to answer these questions below will help you improve your trading game:

1. Why are you entering a trade?
2. Why are you entering at that price?
3. Why are you risking that much?
4. Why are you putting your target at a certain level?

Market Sentiment (Projecting direction)

Nothing will confuse you more than trading without any ideas or understanding of market conditions. In a bullish trending market, we expect more buying opportunities than selling opportunities. While in a bearish trending market we expect more selling opportunities than buying opportunities. As a trader you need to have an idea about the instruments you want to trade or invest in.

We already mentioned different techniques that can be used to trade the market, and now we understand that we need some confluences before anything. These are the following tools that can be used to project your next target:

1. ABCD CYCLE
2. Monthly low and high closing
3. Gauging currency strength
4. Trendline

Projection price and target.

After you've entered a trade you will need to have a target, without one, it would be like driving somewhere without a destination. Projecting price will help you to calculate your risk and as well as where you expect the price to go.

Fibonacci extension

Normally after ABC has been identified, D will be due and will be our next target. The Fibonacci tool will help us to project it, by looking at -38.20% and -61.20%.

Entries

Many traders know how to do analyses but the execution can be challenging.

1. 1-5 structure - serves as an entry structure
2. 123 Market behavior
3. Fade of momentum

Retracements

Retracements are complex and require more patience - this is where most traders lose a lot of money.

1. (C)

A complex retracement normally happens from B to C, obviously no one really knows which level C can be found, but the Fibonacci tool can give us some estimations.

2. Fibonacci retracement levels

a) 38.20%

b) 50.0%

c) 61.8%

Reversal zones

Reversal zones are often where price can change direction.

1. Supply and Demand.
2. Support and resistance.

Here are confluences that you need to consider before you can think of taking any trade.

Weekly timeframe

REVERSAL ZONE

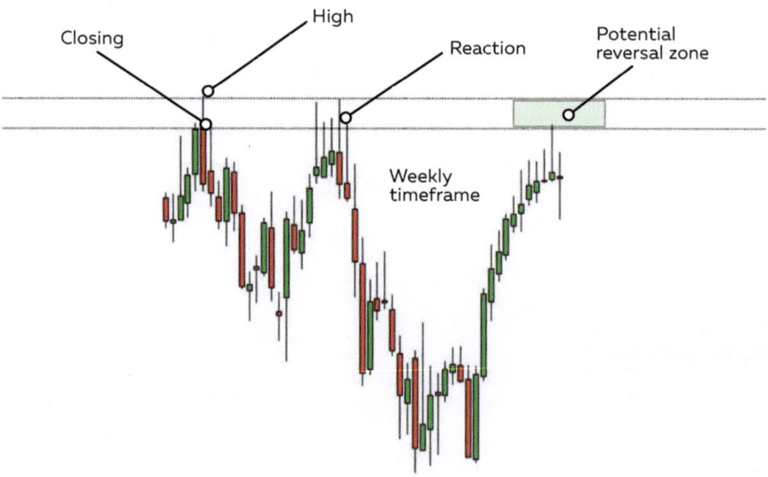

Recapping from chapter one (support and resistance section),using wicks and opening/closing of the candle.

Here we have our reversal zone and 123 is in play with a divergent on the daily timeframe.

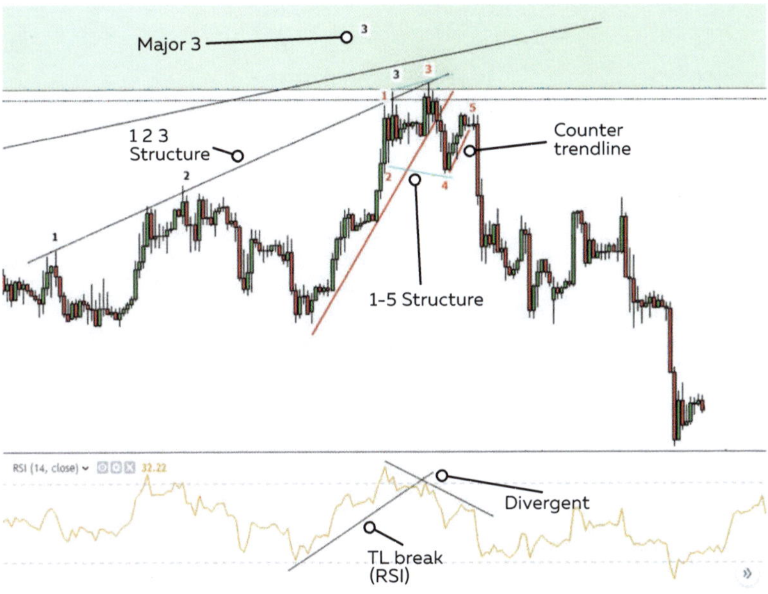

Level 3 is our second layer of divergent when you switch to smaller timeframes and there is another 123 that creates 3. Watch for a divergent and start to look for the 1-5 structure.

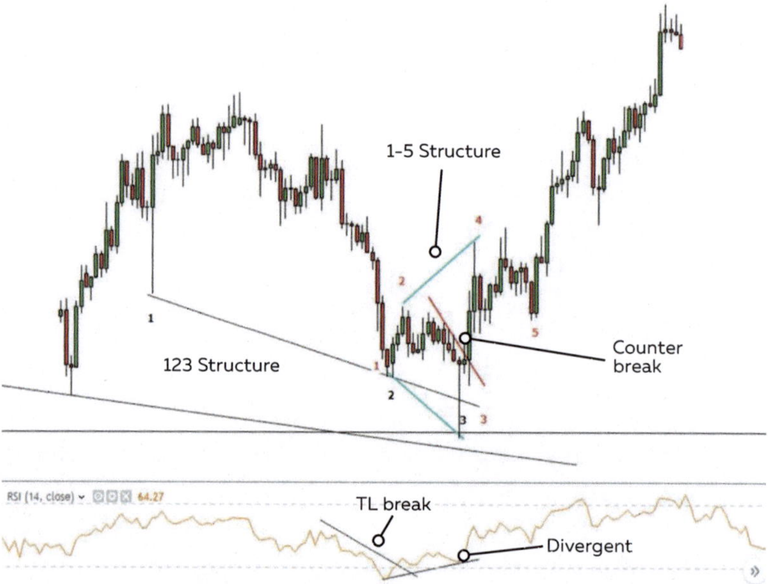

Confluences

1. Weekly reversal
2. Divergent h4
3. 1 2 3 structures
4. 1-5 structure

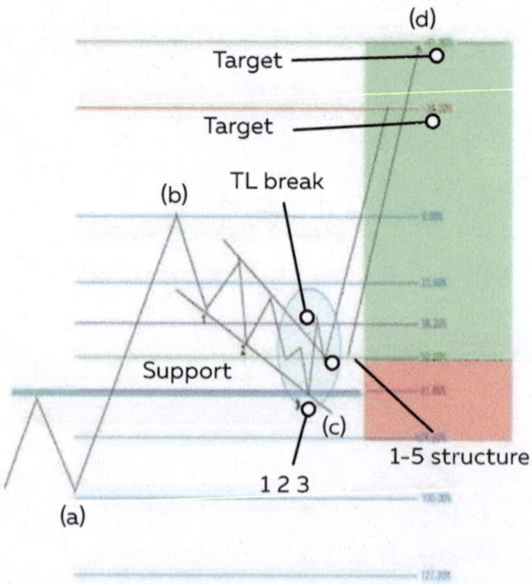

Other examples

Confluences

1. Support
2. ABCD
3. 123 market behavior.
4. 61.8%Fibonacci retracement
5. 1-5 structure

The are many things that need to be considered. In the picture below, we have a lot of confluences that will help you further to better read and understand the market. We have highs being created, an inner and main trendline in play. A break of an inner trendline with a counter trendline break for a sell trade, to main trendline while completing an ABCD pattern probably before buying again at the third touch of a main trendline.

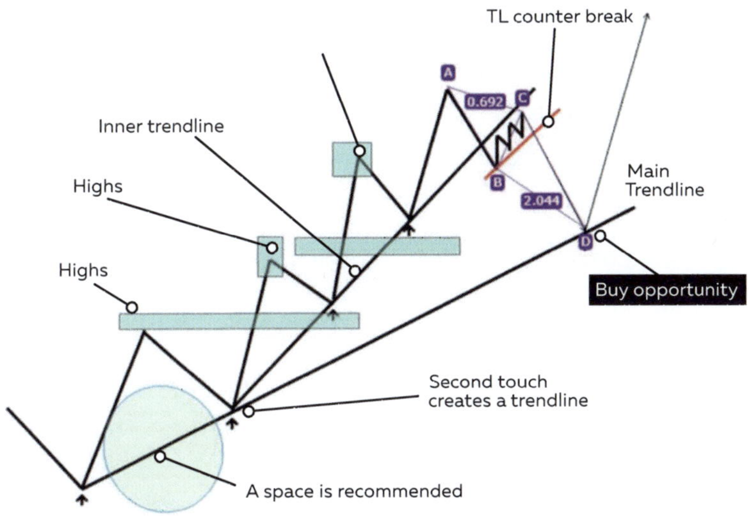

GUIDELINES

Psychology and risk management

Many traders don't talk about psychology. Maybe it's because we are in a rush to make money, we often forget how important it is to be mentally fit. Astute traders change one strategy to another every now and then.

How many times have you doubled or tripled your account and ended up giving back all the money to the market or even more than you've gained? The thing is most traders think about is making money now but not for the long run. This kind of fast approach has damaged more traders than we can imagine. Losing money can affect you psychologically especially if you lose your last savings. Some traders find it hard to let it go – and that's the reason why many traders drop out the market.

The problem is these traders trade on hope, the hope of getting the money they've lost in the past. They take unnecessary risk and overlook analysing the market properly. Trading with emotions makes you impatient and you make more mistakes - closing too early and holding big losses for too long. There is no logic in that, just emotions. You don't need a working system that's 100% to be profitable or sustainable in this business. All you need is proper risk management. The goal is to risk small and gain about twice of what you've risked.

Rules

- Don't confuse yourself with too many thoughts, just look for the ideal setup that meets your requirements
- Don't ever change your rules to meet your needs
- A risk taker doesn't interfere with the risk and process
- Don't hope and pray, just follow your system
- You can't control the market but you can control yourself
- Self-image and confidence influences everything in life
- Poor management of oneself will lead to poor money management
- If you allow your emotions to interfere with your trading, the game is over. Keep everything in writing
- You need to analyze yourself more than you analyze the market
- People who think in groups are not capable of thinking for themselves

Conclusion

Well, we have finally come to the end of the book. I hope this book has given you a far greater understanding of how the market works. Remember that all this information can be improved, trading it is a career, you need passion and patience to have longevity in this field. I believe we are all trying to contribute, even us, we are always students of the market, we are still learning and identifying new things, we learn from other traders and try to discover other missing links from the work of other greater traders in the past. Trading is about personality and how you resonate with a certain styles or other information out there. You must use what makes sense to you, back test it and integrate it with what you currently have or are still going to discover from other sources and create your own system that works for you. At the end of the day it is all about consistency and being profitable despite what are you using.

Acknowledgmenets

First and foremost, I would like to thank to my childhood best friend - Vusi Mtsweni for introducing me to the financial market, the seed you have planted did not fall astray. Thank you man.

I would like to extend my sincere thanks to my mother – Thembi Masilela, who never doubted any ideas that I ever brought up and constantly supported me throughout. Thanks for putting up with me in the dark days. Never forgetting my grandparents who showed love and supported me even when they did not understand what I was doing.

I would like to acknowledge the effort of my childhood best friend - Moses Mahlangu, who has been sharing and working on different ideas, some that never worked but your help and support cannot be overestimated.

Lastly, I would like to express my profound gratitude to my friend, co-author, and business partner – Ref Wayne, your support, encouragement, advice, and determination to make my dream of being an author has come true. I appreciate and thank you, words cannot explain how much I appreciate and am thankful for the collaboration and everything you have done for me.

Many people contributed in many different ways to the completion of this book, and we are most grateful for their efforts.

Printed in Great Britain
by Amazon

76439004R00118